After a brief spell working in the city (London), A M Maxwell qualified as a secondary school teacher and is currently working at a school in Suffolk. Her passion for writing meant that she often wrote her own teaching material, especially to enable lower ability students to access the school curriculum. She has written several articles, short stories and a children's book, *Sick. The Boy Who Refused to Die* is her first full-length book. She has four grown-up children, two grown-up step-children and lives with her husband, Glynn, a primary school teacher, in a small Suffolk village. In rare moments of spare time, she enjoys reading, films, theatre, cooking, cycling and spending time with friends and family.

For Stuart and Mark

A M Maxwell

THE BOY WHO REFUSED TO DIE

AUSTIN MACAULEY PUBLISHERS™

LONDON • CAMBRIDGE • NEW YORK • SHARJAH

A CIP catalogue record for this title is available from the British Library.

ISBN 9781528990875 (Paperback)
ISBN 9781528990882 (Hardback)
ISBN 9781528990899 (ePub e-book)

www.austinmacauley.com

First Published (2020)
Austin Macauley Publishers Ltd
25 Canada Square
Canary Wharf
London
E14 5LQ

My thanks go to the Walsh and Dobinson families for their time and patience whilst I researched Alby's story and especially for the laughs over dinner whilst trying to put this book together. Also, to my husband, Glynn, for introducing me to Alby, helping with the photographs and supplying endless cups of tea to keep me going. I would also like to thank the team at Austin Macauley for the excellent decision that this book was worthy of publication.

Chapter 1
And So It Begins

Sunday, 16 December 2007

"I knew you would want to know, that's all," said Torie as she turned to leave the house.

"That's fine. I'm glad you told me. He's actually with Charlie out playing this afternoon and he knows how I feel about it! I'll speak to him and Charlie as soon as they get back. Don't worry about telling me. Really, I'm glad you did." Lisa smiled but inside she was not happy. In fact, she was more than not happy – she was furious and Alby would know all about it when he got home. Lisa went straight to the playing field and brought Jimmy, Alby and Charlie home. The boys tumbled into the house, laughing and gasping for ⸱ drink. "I need a word with you two," said Lisa, fixing them ⸱ ⸱th with her 'pay attention or else' stare. "Tom's mum's bee ⸱ound this afternoon and she told me she saw both of you c⸱ ⸱ng the road at the traffic lights! Alby, how many times do I ⸱ ⸱ to tell you that you use the underpass? You DON'T cross that road! It's dangerous. The traffic is fast and, apart from anything else, because there's an underpass, drivers don't expect to see pedestrians there. Alby, Charlie, are you listening to me? Do you understand just how serious this is? I want you to tell me that you DO understand how serious it is and you WILL be using that underpass, every single time you cross that road, starting tomorrow!"

"OK, Mum," said Alby, grinning at Charlie. "Mum, do I *have* to go in tomorrow? It is *my* last day and we won't be doing any work anyway. We always have games and mess about. It's not worth it really."

"No," said Lisa, "A school day is a school day and, of course, you've got to go. You'll be home before anyone else on Tuesday anyway. You won't be at the orthodontist that long."

The last day of school was the following Tuesday but Alby had an appointment with the orthodontist in the morning and, as the school was finishing at mid-day, he wouldn't be returning to school after his appointment. That meant that his last day of term was the following day, Monday, 17 December 2007.

Monday, 17 December 2007

Mark

5.30am: Mark dragged himself out of bed and into the shower, grateful that he only had a few days left to work before the Christmas break. Morning rituals completed, he grabbed himself some toast before creeping out of the house and heading off to work – work he enjoyed but he didn't really like the early start. *At least I don't have to compete for the shower*, he thought.

Lisa

7.00am: "Jimmy Dobinson, get out of bed now! You'll be late! Alby's already dressed and having his breakfast. His bus won't wait!" Five minutes later, a bleary-eyed Jimmy appeared at the kitchen door.

"Sorry, Mum," he said. "It's all right for Alby. He doesn't need as much sleep as me. We have to work harder at my school."

"As if," said Alby. "Just wait 'til you get to my school. You'll find out what hard work really is."

Their morning ritual of bustle, banter and being chivvied by Lisa came so naturally to all three that they just took it for granted. It was what happened. It was family. It was life.

"Eat your breakfast, you two, and stop arguing," said Lisa, "or you'll be late." Both boys ate their cereal and toast in virtual silence. Hungry boys have more important things to do than talk. While they breakfasted, Lisa prepared their packed lunches of sandwiches, crisps, a chocolate bar and a drink. She did it every morning and had become so used to it that she thought she could have done it with her eyes closed. Alby also took some money, which he later handed to his friend Tommy. Tommy went to another school but he and Alby met up on the bus coming home and ate the food Tommy had bought for them at Kentucky Fried Chicken.

7.50am: Alby walked out of the house. He turned right and went up to the main road to catch the 608 bus to school. He went with Charlie, Connor, Jordan and Tommy, just as he did every school day.

8.30am: Jimmy walked out of the house. He turned left to go to his local primary school. Lisa had just started letting him walk there on his own, just as she hoped he would every school day.

Lisa closed the front door and went back into the kitchen to clear away the breakfast dishes, just as Mark would do for the next eighteen months.

3.45pm: Lisa was just finishing the ironing when the sound of the front door bell echoed around the house. Barefoot, Lisa opened it and smiled at Alby's friend Charlie. Charlie was breathless. "Alby's had an accident!" Charlie's face was full of messages he couldn't utter. Lisa's mind emptied of every thought as the wave of cold outside air hit her.

"Stay here – Jimmy's due home any minute!" Her body went into overdrive as sprinted out of the house. Her bare feet tore up the pavement as they bore her far too slowly to the top of the road. Cars had stopped. People had stopped. Time had stopped.

The air was forced from her body as she gasped at the figure lying in the middle of the central reservation of the dual carriageway. Somewhere, someone screamed. She ran over and collapsed beside him. She grabbed his hand. "Come on,

Alby, wake up!" she shrieked, being absolutely certain, somewhere deep in the recesses of her mind, that if she shouted loud enough, it would wake him up. *He's just been knocked out – he'll come round in a minute*, she thought. She had no more rational thoughts.

"The ambulance is on its way," someone said. She sat by the central reservation and an icy cold wave washed through her body. She needed to call her dad. Someone handed her a mobile phone but her trembling hands wouldn't hit the right numbers. She couldn't do it. Her fingers wouldn't work. Her mind wouldn't work. What was his number? Her voice wouldn't work properly but she recalled her dad's number from her frozen memory and someone phoned him for her.

Lisa looked at the twisted little figure. He was breathing. His leg was bent under him but there was no blood – Lisa was grateful for that because it meant he wasn't badly hurt. He was alive and that was a good sign, surely, although his breathing wasn't right. She looked at her son. He was still wearing his school rucksack – the rucksack he would fling down when he got home and leave it until Lisa told him to hang it up. How did he end up with his upper body on one side of the barrier and his legs on the other? Where's the ambulance? Where's Dad? My son, my precious, beautiful Alby, please don't die. Please God, don't let him die. He can't die. He's my Alby and you can't let him die.

Someone moved Lisa away and put a duvet around her shoulders. She hadn't felt the cold but she did feel the duvet. Then someone handed her a cup of tea. It was far too sweet.

Mark

3.55pm: Traffic on the M25 was as heavy as usual, but at least it was moving. *It hasn't been nicknamed 'the biggest car park in the world' for nothing*, mused Mark as he realised that he would reach the turning for the A12 in half a mile. As he flicked the indicator left, he started thinking about Christmas. The weather was dry and cold but not freezing. Christmas decorations were everywhere and each year it seemed that more and more people were trying to outdo their neighbours

– expressing their delight with the season of goodwill and demonstrating their Christmas cheer with louder and more garish external decorations. Mark was looking forward to having time away from work and having a proper old-fashioned family Christmas with Lisa and the boys. They hadn't made definite plans about seeing Linda and Jim (Lisa's parents) or Pauline and Bernie (the parents of Lisa's first husband, Scott, and also the other much-loved grandparents of Alby and Jimmy) but he knew that Christmas wouldn't be Christmas without them around too.

4.10pm: Mark suddenly realised that the traffic on the slip road had backed up and he thought that the earlier traffic flow had been too good to be true. Still, home wasn't far and the traffic was at least moving, albeit very slowly. As he travelled down the road, Mark could see the cause of the hold-up. Cars had stopped – some weren't in the right position to be in a traffic queue. Then he saw people clustered around the central reservation and saw them bending over something and then he saw that that something was a person. He turned into his road. Mark thought it was a bit rough for someone to collapse at this time of year. Then he saw Charlie. Charlie was on the doorstep and the door was open. There was no Lisa.

The thunder of Mark's thoughts crashed all around him as the lightning bolt of realisation hit him full in the chest. In the same instant as he realised it was one of the boys he knew it was Alby because Jimmy was at a disco. He didn't remember abandoning the car as he propelled himself towards the top of the road and Lisa. And Alby. Terrified anticipation flowed through him like a torrent. In situations like this, thoughts don't come neatly ordered, one at a time. They pile in with abject disregard for anything or anyone else. *It will destroy Lisa if he's dead! He can't be dead – he's virtually my son too! It's Christmas for God's sake! Where is she? Maybe it's not Alby. Maybe this is a nightmare and I'll be awake soon. Alby can't die! What can I do? What can I say to her? How could I possibly make this better?*

Lisa and Mark

Lisa turned to look at Mark. He didn't remember saying anything to her but he must have done. He saw Alby's twisted little frame lying on that road with his beautiful wife silently pouring wave after wave of the purest love – a mother's love – all over her son. The sight of them tore Mark's heart into pieces.

He tried to cuddle Lisa. "No don't!" she said. Mark understood. Alby needed the cuddles. Perhaps if everyone cuddled him it would save him. The ambulance arrived and Mark watched as they did what they had to do. *I must be strong for Lisa,* he thought, *she needs me.* Then Mark thought, *But I love Alby too, so where do I get my strength from?*

Penny from next door appeared. She wanted to help. People were kind. Penny's son, Dean, would go to the school to fetch Jimmy. Penny would look after Jimmy.

The ambulance crew said Alby's heart was working well but then he kept trying to curl up into the foetal position. Lisa heard one of them say that could mean Alby had suffered a brain injury. She thought she might be sick. Mark helped her into the ambulance and then climbed in too. *We will get through this,* he thought, *we have to,* and the doors closed. Someone was banging on the doors shouting "Let me in!" but the ambulance drove off.

Throughout the relatively short journey, the ambulance crew worked on Alby, their fingers deftly working to keep his airway clear, to monitor his heartbeat to watch for signs of impending crises and they cut off his clothes, revealing massive bruising down his left side.

Queen's Hospital, Romford, Essex. Neurological centre of excellence. Alby was in Accident and Emergency. The well-oiled wheels swung into action and as experienced hands swarmed all over him testing, listening, checking, writing and talking, Lisa could only watch. She prayed that these people would understand just how much she needed them to save Alby's life. There was no question that he could die – on the contrary, that idea was completely out of the question. Utterly unthinkable.

Lisa's sisters, Samantha and Nicola, arrived. They realised very quickly that there was a possibility that Lisa wouldn't consider – that she might lose Alby. Sammy whispered to Nicky, "If anything happens to Alby, it'll kill her!" They grasped each other's hand and clutched the end of the bed, staring at their nephew in disbelief.

This sort of thing happens to other people, but not us, they both thought.

Nicky rang Bernie to tell him to fetch Scott. "Yes," she said, "it is that bad! And get your mum and dad here as quickly as you can!"

One of the ambulance crew guided Lisa to the reception desk to register Alby's details. Lisa opened her mouth and only the word 'Alby' came out. Her legs gave way and the lovely ambulance man (as Lisa later remembered him) held her. Then she gave way to anguished sobs of pure despair and her mind gave way to hope. She looked up and saw her mum and dad. Jim put his arms round her and the sobbing took control of Lisa once more. They were in the best place.

Lisa and Mark stood at the end of the bed, stunned. Jim had his arm round his daughter. Neither of them spoke. Alby was taken away for X-rays and scans. Bit by bit, the events and the consequences of that afternoon were unfolding. Alby had stepped into the road and the driver of the car that had hit him just hadn't seen him. Why had Alby stepped into the road? Why hadn't the driver seen him? They would never know the answer to either of those questions.

Alby's leg was broken in three places. That would heal. His body had rolled and his brain had obviously rolled with it. His body had stopped but his brain had continued to move and as a consequence of this he had dozens of tiny bleeds in his brain. The skull is sharp on the inside and the continuous motion caused by the accident tore at his brain tissue.

Jim

4.20pm: Jim was looking forward to Christmas with his family when the phone rang. "Alby's been run over at the top of the road!"

"I'll be there!" he whispered as he dropped the phone and time stood still for him.

He rang Linda and told her what had happened.

He couldn't remember the drive from Hornchurch to Lisa's road but he arrived just as the ambulance doors were closing. Jim leapt out of his car and raced to the ambulance. He pounded on the doors shouting, "Let me in!" but the ambulance didn't stop. It powered through the traffic to take its precious cargo to hospital. This was an emergency Jim had always thought happened to other families. He put his hands up to his in despair as the ambulance drove off.

Linda

Linda had been shopping. Not ordinary, boring shopping but Christmas shopping. Thoughts of Christmas and the presents she had bought for her family filled her mind. For her, watching their delight as they unwrapped the surprises she had planned for them was an important part of Christmas. She thought she had chosen well and was feeling at peace with the world – even though she still had so much to do in the few days left before the rushing around ceased and everyone could breathe a sigh of relief, ready to just enjoy being with their families. Her mobile phone rang and broke her train of thought. It was Jim. She listened to his words and raw, cold disbelief enveloped her. "Alby's been run over," he had said. Linda's knuckles turned white as she gripped the steering wheel. She stared through the windscreen and in an anguished whisper said, "Oh no. Not again."

Saturday, 27 September 1958

Linda's mum turned as she left. "Make sure you peel the potatoes and do the other veg for dinner while I'm out please and don't let Gary eat too many sweets." Mum worked at Victor Value's Supermarket. She had to go and Linda was in charge. Dad had probably been at work in Rotherhithe, London, for over an hour already. Her sister, Pat, was out. She was fifteen and she was more or less allowed to do what she wanted – well, during the day, anyway.

"Yes, Mum," her youngest daughter replied. Linda was busy. She didn't mind though. She liked helping her mum with the other children. Dad said that children "grow up so fast these days" and he was right. Linda had a fair bit of responsibility for an eleven-year-old but it wasn't uncommon for children to look after younger siblings – both at home and outside. Her brother, Jeffrey, didn't need looking after. He'd been going out with his friends for a long time. Their world wasn't particularly dangerous, especially during the day. You had to watch out at night though. Linda tried not to get caught outside after dark and sometimes she ran so fast to get home before nightfall that her little lungs nearly burst. Some of the men who'd had too much to drink at the local pub could be terrifying. As an adult, Linda realised they were probably harmless, but to a young girl they were very frightening.

Linda busied herself with the chores her mum had left her. Jeffrey said, "Tar-ar sis. I'm off. We're going to the pictures. See you later," and with that the door slammed and he was gone. Linda couldn't help thinking it was a bit unfair that girls had to do 'stuff' at home but boys pretty much got away without having to do very much except tidy up their bedrooms occasionally. Jeffrey and his friends were off to the Carlton Picture House. *Lucky beggars*, thought Linda but reminded herself that she might have a bit of time to herself before her mum returned so she set about the remainder of her chores with renewed energy.

Mum came back and not long afterwards someone knocked on the door. Usually, Linda could hear her mum chatting animatedly to the caller, or they'd come through into the sitting room. But there was nothing. The silence seemed to last forever before she heard a low, anguished sob tear itself from her mother. The lady from next door was the next person to enter the sitting room and she told Linda that she'd have to come with her 'for a bit'. Linda wondered about that. For a bit of what? Cake? Dinner? She looked at the lady's face but saw nothing except an expression that said, "Don't ask. Please don't ask."

The lady was kind and Linda found her older sister Pat and little Gary were also there. Linda looked around her. It was the same type of house as the one that she and her family lived in but it looked completely different. It was decorated differently and had different furniture. *It makes a big difference to how the house looks*, thought Linda. Then her mum came into the room. She gathered her children around her. She didn't look right. It seemed to Linda that she held her breath – as if she didn't know what to say. Then Linda thought her mum looked confused as she put her arms round them, drawing them closer to her. They were all there but not Dad. And not Jeffrey. Where was Jeffrey? The film should have finished hours ago. "I've something to tell you," said Mum, "and I don't know how to. We all have to be very brave and very strong, for each other and especially for Dad…" Her voice tailed off as she sobbed and put her head in her hands. "There's been a terrible accident and…" she hesitated once more. "Oh darlings, our Jeffrey was knocked down by a car today and he was so badly hurt he… he's not coming back, I'm afraid." Linda knew Jeffrey was dead. Mum didn't actually say that awful word but she might well have done. Linda was only 11 but she knew what it meant.

Linda pieced together what had happened – mostly from listening to grown-ups. Jeffrey had been with his friends. No one knew why, but he had stepped out into the path of an oncoming car in Essex Road. He had briefly regained consciousness, said, "Oh no," and then died.

Linda gripped the steering wheel and then brushed the tears from her cheek. This was 1958 all over again.

Jimmy

Jimmy had been at a school Christmas disco. He had made lots of friends of his own age and he was having a great time, stuffing himself with sweets and generally messing around with his mates. He saw Dean from next door come into the hall and speak to one of the teachers. The teacher peered over the heads of the excited children and made a beeline for Jimmy. She guided him out of the hall and told him that he needed to leave. He went back with Dean back to Penny's house, feeling bewildered. They told him Alby had had an accident but didn't give him any details. They told him that Mum and Mark were at the hospital. He sat watching TV at their house, not knowing what to say. They were very kind to him, but Jimmy felt wrong being there. If something horrible had happened, he wanted to be with his family.

At half past five, Charlie's big brother, Tom, came to collect Jimmy and took him to Queen's Hospital. Lisa decided that he should be allowed to see Alby. She could not be sure what the next few hours or days would bring and deep down she wondered if Jimmy would ever have the chance to see Alby again.

He was kind too, but Jimmy sensed that Tom didn't know what to say to him. He thought that Alby would probably have a big bandage somewhere and possibly a black eye. Nothing prepared him for what he saw – wires, tubes, bleeping machines, whispers, lots of grown-ups, shouting, crying. And Alby. Alby had gone off to school. It was going to be Christmas soon. Jimmy and Alby would have mega presents. They always did. Everyone would be there. It would be brilliant. But this wasn't brilliant. He cried. Lots. "Alby never looked where he was going," he told Lisa. "He should have looked! Don't worry, Mum, he'll be all right," and he touched Lisa's arm. With that, hot, anxious tears of love engulfed Lisa's face as she watched the wretched figure of her eldest son and prayed for him to survive. Jim wanted to help his daughter and he needed to do something practical. People always say 'let me know if there's anything I can do' in situations like this and he knew that the best thing he could do for Lisa would be to look after Jimmy. At midnight, he took young Jimmy home.

Scott

Scott had arrived at the hospital. Conflict and argument were forgotten. Scott hugged Lisa as he looked at their son.

Ten months earlier, Lisa had stopped smoking. Scott never had stopped. That night the two of them made nicotine their crutch as they stepped outside the hospital to draw deep breaths of the night air, to draw deep breaths from nicotine-laden cigarettes and to draw the deep breaths of exhaustion.

"...so we need to transfer him to Great Ormond Street – now," they told her. Queen's Hospital is a neurological centre of excellence – but not if you're a child. It's only a neurological centre of excellence if you're an adult. *What's the difference*? Lisa thought angrily, fearful that the delay might affect Alby adversely. She wanted him treated, put right, made well, there and then. She didn't want the delay that the move would inevitably mean. She later discovered that the staff at Queen's wanted Alby to be transferred to Great Ormond Street in a helicopter but it couldn't land on the busy A12.

Lisa never remembered getting into the ambulance again. She couldn't take her eyes off Alby for one moment. *If he opens his eyes, I want him to know I am there for him – always,* she thought. Lisa remembered the enormity of the love that only a mother can feel for her child. She spoke silently of her willingness to change places with him, to give him a chance, to die for him if she had to. Then angry grief appeared from nowhere and slowly wrapped his pernicious arms around her as she silently screamed "WHY?" There was no reply.

Lisa went with Alby. She went with the nurses monitoring him. She went with the medical equipment which was probably keeping him alive – the tubes, the masks and the needles. She went with a mother's burning need for her child to live and she went with Scott. They only allowed parents in the ambulance, which Lisa thought was ludicrous. Scott hadn't seen Lisa for two years – not that this was the time or place for recriminations but she realised this 'parents only' rule would hurt Mark, who'd been a brilliant stepfather to Alby. Lisa knew Alby would have wanted her, Mark *and* Scott to be there for him. Lisa corrected herself, "No, it's what he wants – he *wants* us not to argue and to be there for him and now we are." But she wished that the circumstances of the unity between her and Scott had been different.

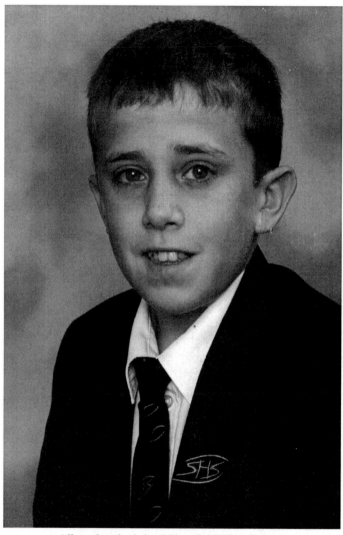

Alby when he joined Shenfield High School

Chapter 2

Great Ormond
Street Children's Hospital

17 December 2007

11.00pm: Great Ormond Street Hospital: Several members of staff in the London children's hospital were waiting for them. A special blanket and a fan were produced. Lisa was told that Alby would be sedated for at least a week and he would need to be kept cool. She felt comforted by the perpetual motion generated by the hospital staff. Doctors and nurses all knew their parts and were playing them seamlessly. They were all focussed on Alby and Lisa was reassured. She had finally stopped crying when someone said she would have to leave the room. Doctors were going to drill into Alby's head to measure the pressure on his brain. She gasped with terror. Hadn't his little head been through enough? *Drill! You drill teeth or roads! You don't drill my beautiful child's skull!* As Lisa's hand flew over her mouth, Mark and Scott led her out of the room.

A hundred years later, a doctor appeared out of the mists of Lisa's worst imaginings. "The pressure in Alby's head is normal and we've inserted a monitor to keep an eye on it. The last thing we want at the moment is for Alby's brain to start swelling. We just have to wait now." And wait they did.

Lisa and Scott spent the longest night of their lives by Alby's bed. Staff gently suggested that they get some rest but neither of them had the slightest inclination to leave their vigil. Even going for a drink seemed like tempting fate – what if Alby needed either of them and they weren't there? *Suppose*

Alby takes a turn for the worse or even wakes up and asks for me, she thought, completely forgetting that the sedation would ensure he didn't wake up just yet.

Lisa's body ached with exhaustion and her shredded emotions wove themselves into every corner of her brain. What if? What if? What if? A myriad of questions, all starting the same way, pressed themselves onto her. Dawn broke quietly outside as the sounds of a hospital gearing up for the day's work filtered through her tangled thoughts. Questions that she would be asking for years after this night starting forming in her numbed brain. Why did she make him go to school that day? How did it happen? What was that driver *doing* that meant she didn't see Alby and his friends? Why didn't Alby use the underpass to cross that wretched road?

Nobody thought about practical things, like where would the family sleep? Who was allowed to stay at the hospital? They stayed in the hospital's Family Room but Lisa was stunned when she was told that the hospital would allow Scott, as Alby's father, to stay in the room but not Mark. Eventually, the family was given a room at the nearby Italian Hospital. Built in 1884 specifically to help Italian immigrants who faced language problems in other English hospitals, it had long since ceased to be used as a hospital but provided invaluable accommodation to the families of patients in Great Ormond Street Hospital. Scott stayed in the Family Room.

18 December 2007

7.30am: Mark took Lisa, Scott and Linda to a café outside the hospital. Lisa knew she should eat something and thought she couldn't swallow her sausage sandwich because it was so dry. Maybe it was just a dreadful sandwich but maybe she just didn't want to eat. Eating was a normal thing to do and there was no way Lisa could act normally whilst Alby was lying in that hospital, fighting for his life.

9.30am: Lisa suddenly realised that she ought to let her employers know what had happened. She thought it was strange that this catastrophic thing had descended on her and her family but everybody else was carrying on as if nothing had happened. Linda rang Lisa's work colleague, another Lisa, at Canary Wharf and within half an hour, a car brought Lisa 2 to the hospital. She burst into tears when she saw the family looking so tired and wretched. Lisa 2 said that no one would be expecting Lisa to return to work and she should just concentrate on being there for Alby and Jimmy. It was all she could do.

The first consultant to enter Lisa's life walked into the room at 8.30am. "We are concerned about Alby's heart. We think he may have a torn aorta. If it is as we suspect, he will need an operation and I think it only fair to warn you that he may not survive the surgery. Alby has to be seen by a heart specialist first and we'll take it from there." Lisa didn't wonder how much worse it could get. She already knew.

10.30am: Lisa's dad, Jim, had left Queen's hospital and returned home to look after young Jimmy. On the way home he had pondered on the devastation caused to so many people by the day's events. Lisa *had* to be with Alby. She would be there for Jimmy later but, for the time being at least, someone needed to be there for Jimmy and Jim would be that person. Thanks to there being a station at Harold Wood, it didn't take Jimmy and Jim long to arrive at Great Ormond Street. The moment Lisa saw her dad, she wanted to tell him how scared she was about Alby having the heart operation but she couldn't articulate the words through the tears. Tears that she would have sworn came from a place that was all cried out. They flowed in torrents and choked her. She could only get the words out in fits and starts. "Let's just wait love," said Jim, "and see what the heart specialist says."

11.00am: Mark's sister Lynne and her friend Charlotte arrived. Not wanting to interrupt anything, Lynn had texted Mark, "We're downstairs." Mark went to see them and explained what had happened.

Lynne broke down. "Oh no, Mark," she sobbed, "it's just too awful for words."

"We just have to wait and see," said Mark, "there's nothing else we can do."

12.10pm: The heart specialist appeared in the doorway. With the light behind her, someone with an over-active imagination could easily have mistaken her for an angel. Lisa daren't let her imagination take control. She had never imagined she'd be in the position she was in that morning and imagination was, therefore, dangerous. As the specialist spoke, Lisa felt the tears in her throat and on her face – again. Alby's heart was absolutely fine and there would be no need to operate. Alby's heartbeat was strong.

Hospitals have changed. No secrecy now. Staff explain what they are doing or what they are going to do and so began the first of an interminable list of procedures and plans that the hospital intended carrying out. Alby would remain sedated for the time being to give his brain a chance to stabilise and his body a chance to heal itself. He was attached to a ventilator to minimise the effort that his body had to expend. Lisa knew that if you were really poorly bed rest was the best way to heal. That is what they were giving Alby – the chance to heal. An intravenous line kept up his fluid levels and machines monitored all his other levels.

19 December 2007

The pneumococcus bacteria that causes pneumonia usually manages to take hold when the body's immune system is compromised – fighting other infections or injuries. Therefore it came as no surprise to the nurses when Alby developed pneumonia. His lungs were badly affected and he was given powerful antibiotics intravenously. No one knew if they would work – Alby's life was still hanging in the balance. So congested were Alby's lungs that staff were convinced that he was a heavy smoker. In fact, Alby actually detested everything about cigarettes and had never touched them. He required physiotherapy to release the mucus to enable him to breathe and Lisa became distressed every time she saw the manipulation of his shattered body. He was pounded, prodded and pulled in every direction. But it worked and the infection gradually left him.

Jimmy became friendly with Maddy. Maddy's brother, Keller, was in the bed next to Alby. Maddy filled the gap left by Alby, and Jimmy filled the gap left by Keller. It was a mutually beneficial and supportive arrangement into which the two children fell with an ease that only the innocence of childhood can achieve.

20 December 2007

Lisa sat by Alby's bed and held his hand. Then she stroked his hand, silently and then not-so-silently willing him to recover, to get better, to end this living hell. The device on his head was still measuring the pressure in his brain, which was not giving cause for concern. His broken leg was still held immobile pending the surgery it needed. Lisa was allowed to attend to a little of Alby's physical care – she was allowed to brush his teeth and wash his face. Sometimes she didn't need a bowl of water to do this. The tears she shed would have provided more than enough to give him a bath, let alone a face wash.

21 December 2007

Charlie, Connor, Jake and Tom came to the hospital with Tom's mum, Torie, and Charlie's mum, Tracey. Alby's friends were all 12 years old and to minimise trauma for them a photograph was taken of Alby and the friends were counselled by a play therapist in order to prepare them for seeing him. Alby's friends were quiet as they looked at the helpless figure of their friend.

Alby had been heavily sedated when they put an incontinence pad on him. Lisa felt for him. *He doesn't know anything about it*, she thought, *but he'd hate having that thing on him.*

Someone suggested the incontinence pad should say 'Gucci' so Lisa took a black marker and wrote on it in large black letters. They all laughed. Lisa smiled at the humour. It marked the point at which she saw a glimmer of something like the fun that had filled her previous life. That life, for the time being, was a distant memory and would always be different. Last Monday, she had thought that she would never laugh again – but you have to, eventually.

Alby had to go to theatre. The major concern had been his brain but he also had many physical injuries that needed attention. His left leg was broken in three places and had to have a metal bar inserted to stabilise it. His left arm was broken above and below the elbow and this, too, required the insertion of a plate.

He was returned to the Intensive Care Unit and attempts were made to feed him but he couldn't take nutrition into his stomach and it was discovered that he had pancreatitis. His pancreas was badly bruised but not torn. A nasal gastro line was inserted through Alby's nose and into his stomach. Lisa winced as they inserted it and hoped that it didn't hurt him. Lisa looked at the frailness of Alby's body. He had been through so much but he had fought back.

"At least he can start really getting better now that those operations are out of the way," she told Mark. Then Alby deteriorated.

24 December 2007

"We're going to reduce Alby's sedation today, Lisa," said the consultant. "We think it's time to see whether he can cope on his own and the withdrawal of the sedation will probably wake him up." Lisa was overjoyed. She knew this was the first opportunity that she would have to make him understand how much he was loved. She wanted to hold his hand, to talk to him and to hug him. Gradually, Alby's sedation and his dependence on the ventilator were reduced. His heartbeat was still strong and soon he was breathing on his own. Everyone waited. But Alby didn't wake up. Lisa looked at the nurses, then at the doctor, then at Mark. "Why isn't he waking up?" she asked but no one replied. "Why isn't he waking up?" she shouted.

"We don't know, Lisa," said the doctor. "These things take time. His heartbeat and breathing are strong, so we now have to just wait and see what happens. There are different levels of unconsciousness and at the moment we don't know which level we may be dealing with." Lisa knew nothing about levels of unconsciousness. She just couldn't understand why Alby's heart and lungs were strong and working as they should but the rest of him wasn't. Eventually, he opened his eyes but there was no recognition of anyone or anything. Alby was exactly the same as when he'd been unconscious.

Jimmy wanted to stay in London. He didn't want to go home and leave his brother. He didn't want to leave his mum and Mark. He didn't want to leave in case something else awful happened. He just *had* to be there with them all. Jimmy couldn't stay at the Italian Hospital as it just wasn't safe. It had open stairwells, which 21st-century planning laws wouldn't permit. However, as 21st-century users were living in a 19th-century building with all its peculiarities and dangers, the provision of family accommodation became of paramount importance.

Enter, the Sick Children's Trust. Neither Lisa nor Mark had ever heard of this charity but they were speechless with joy when they were offered much-needed accommodation in a house in nearby Grays Inn Road, where they would be able to stay together and be near Alby. They later discovered that the actor Michael Crawford was the Chairman of the Sick Children's Trust, whose motto is 'We're here so you can be there'. Lisa and Mark described the Trust as a Godsend. They took up residence in Grays Inn Road and Scott moved to the Italian Hospital. He could be trusted with 19th-century open stairwells.

September 1994

Lisa

They had lied to her. They had all lied to her and she wouldn't forget it in a hurry. She would exact her revenge – how she didn't yet know – but she would, and they would all be sorry. For the time being, though, she had something else which was taking all her attention, draining all her energy and shattering the rose-coloured spectacles through which she had been viewing that day.

Lisa stared at the hospital walls – they looked depressed. Cracking, peeling, tired paintwork, clinging to the walls as though in desperation to continue its useful life, even though this hospital had come to the end of its life. Lisa knew it had been given the thumbs down. It was not wanted, finished, not useful anymore and the decision had been made – it had to go. Lisa thought, *It's funny that this hospital is dying when I am bringing it new life...* but her thoughts were cut short as another excruciating wall of pain crushed her under its weight. She cursed her best friend, she cursed her mum and her mum's best friend, she cursed the lady in the corner shop, her doctor, the doctor's receptionist, the midwife, the ambulance crew and nurse who admitted her to the hospital four hours ago. They were all liars. Smilingly, they had referred to 'backache, mild discomfort and period-type pain'. Not one of them had prepared her for what was happening to her now. If someone up there had decided that her time was up, well she'd rather not have to go through this indescribable pain first – 'please God, just let me die!' she'd pleaded but no one was listening and the pain continued. She clenched the mask delivering gas and air as if her life depended on it – she thought that it actually did.

She didn't know how long she would have to wait for this first baby of hers to put in an appearance and she was able to drift off into realms she rarely had time to visit. Lisa and Scott had been together for six years. They'd met in '88 at a The Aspen Tree, Collier Row's place-to-be pub and Lisa thought Scott was a complete idiot. She thought his unkempt hair looked awful, his clothes were a joke and she thought he wore far too much after-shave. Scott saw Lisa and though she was the fittest bird he'd ever seen. He turned on the charm tap and Lisa drowned.

One day, as they climbed into his car, he said, "I'm taking you home to meet Mum and Dad," Scott's parents lived in Hornchurch. As they pulled up outside the neatly dressed windows of a small semi-detached house, Lisa's giggles erupted and she couldn't stop them. "What on earth's got into you?" Scott asked.

"The downstairs curtain of that house is moving and there's a *man's* nose on the windowsill!" Scott didn't sound surprised when he said,

"That's my place and it's probably Dad checking you out. He's asked me loads of questions about you."

"I thought that's what mums did, not dads! Let's hope I'm good enough for his little boy then... come on, let's get inside and get on with it."

Bernie and Pauline were completely taken with Lisa. "What a cracker," Bernie said later to Pauline.

"She's a lovely girl, Bernie, our Scott's done well for himself. It's good to see him so happy and I get the impression she's the sort of girl who won't take any nonsense. He needs someone like her."

July 1993

Lisa and Scott stood outside the semi-detached house in Harold Wood. A rush of excitement enveloped them as they looked at their new home. Lisa squeezed Scott's hand. "What are you thinking?" she asked.

"I am wondering what on earth we've done, buying this place," said Scott. "It's worse than I remembered it and I'd like to get it finished before I retire!" Lisa laughed with only a slightly nervous edge to her voice.

"That's why it was so cheap, you nutter, and the sooner we start the quicker it'll be finished."

The property that Lisa and Scott had bought was a wreck. The 1930s' house needed so much work that Lisa's 'quicker' actually materialised into three years, which, she supposed, was quicker than, say, nine or ten years. The ceilings and windows needed replacing. There was a possibility that the false beams in the ceiling contained asbestos, so they would need to be replaced. Everywhere was in desperate need of paint and new carpets. The only toilet was attached to the house but it had no direct access from the house. It was situated on the outside rear wall, which was accessed via the kitchen door to the garden and a few feet to the right, under a shabby plastic cover. Having an internal toilet became a priority. The bathroom was located next to the kitchen in the rear of the house and the living room occupied the front part of the house. Three bedrooms upstairs completed Lisa and Scott's first home.

The house remained a 'work in progress' for over three years. The third bedroom was turned into a bathroom and the old bathroom and toilet were incorporated into the kitchen, transforming it into a comfortable kitchen/diner. Lisa continued to work in London as a settlements clerk, which meant that they could only work on the house at weekends and the work was slow and far from finished when Lisa eventually went into hospital. She was dragged back from the past by the sound of screaming and the knowledge that her abdomen was definitely being torn into a hundred pieces.

Alby

Alby James Dobinson was born on 22 September 1994. Lisa thought he was amazing. So perfect. His finger and toenails were absolute perfection. So was his nose. And his mouth. And those little ears were the most beautiful ears that any baby anywhere in the world ever had! She was so lucky. Lisa needn't have worried about sleepless nights because she didn't have them. From day one, Alby was the perfect baby. He was happy, contented and slept. When he wasn't sleeping, he was smiling. The house was by no means finished and Lisa sat Alby on top of the tumble dryer, in his baby chair, whilst work continued on the living room. Alby's appearance made them work faster in an attempt to complete the renovation of the house before they retired. Linda ended up telling her daughter to have another baby so that they would be encouraged to work even faster on the house, as Alby's appearance seemed to have spurred them on.

As Alby grew, he delighted in everything with which he came into contact. His contented nature and infectious smile won the hearts of all who saw him. Lisa thought infectious was a strange word to describe something as beautiful as a baby's smile, but you could certainly catch something from her baby and that was pure love. Adored by his parents and grandparents, Alby soon carved out his niche in their hearts. His favourite toy was Thomas the Tank Engine and he played contentedly with his Thomas set day after day.

Lisa returned to work as a settlements clerk with Leemans in London and Alby was looked after by her mother, Linda.

Jimmy

Jimmy Scott Dobinson was born on the ninth of September 1996. His older brother was fascinated by this little bundle that kept making a noise. He looked at him, smiled at him and prodded him, showing no signs of jealousy or irk. He just loved his baby brother from day one and quickly established the bond for which the two boys were to become well known. Eventually, the bundle smiled back at him and Alby liked that. As the bundle began growing and sitting, Alby liked to entertain him. He'd give him toys to play with and pick them up when they were dropped.

As the years passed, Alby and Jimmy became inseparable. Alby and his shadow became a familiar sight in the area of their home. They played together and everyone thought it surprising that they didn't argue. They simply loved each other and loved being with each other.

Nothing changed when Jimmy eventually joined Alby at Harold Court Primary School. Alby's friends became Jimmy's friends. At break-time, Jimmy was always included in the game of football being played by Alby and his mates. Alby's friends accepted Jimmy as readily as they accepted Alby. Jimmy never acted two years younger than the others, which probably made it much easier for them all to accept him. Then, staff at the school began to worry. The time was fast approaching for Alby to leave primary school and begin his new life at secondary school. Staff feared that Jimmy would be bereft without Alby, so began encouraging Jimmy to mix with children of his own age. He was an adaptable young man but did miss his brother when Alby went to Shenfield High School. However, outside school he still played with Alby and his friends and later, as they all grew into their teens, Alby's friends still acknowledged Jimmy as one of their friends and not just Alby's younger brother.

Work on the house progressed and it had become a comfortable family home. Alby and Jimmy were both at school but just as Lisa thought that life couldn't get any better she realised that she and Scott had been growing apart for years and in May 2003 they separated. They'd been spending a great deal of time apart and it seemed inevitable. The boys would visit Scott's parents and Scott would see them there. Contact between Lisa and Scott became non-existent and Lisa settled into life as a single parent. The separation morphed into divorce. Lisa hadn't planned that. It wasn't what was supposed to happen. Life wasn't fair but she had no choice but to go with it. On the outside, she was resilient and capable and she did her very best to provide Alby and Jimmy with everything they needed – not just materially but Lisa gave them vitally important emotional security and stability. On the inside, she felt that they'd all been let down but she decided that her boys would never feel let down. She'd make sure of it.

25 December 2007

Lisa watched the grey light of dawn filtering through the curtains. She knew for sure that this was all real but, somewhere in the deep recesses of yesterday, she still hoped that the boys would run into her bedroom and jump on the bed yelling "Wake up, Mum, it's Christmas!" She would, of course, open her eyes and shudder with relief that it had all been a nightmare – *Just like in Dickens' Christmas Carol,* she thought. As she turned over, she realised that her pillow was damp.

Alby and Jimmy had fantastic Christmas presents awaiting them at home in Harold Wood. The boys were to have a flat screen TV and DVD player. Scott had bought them a Play Station. Their fantastic Christmas presents stayed wrapped until Easter. Lisa took a few "useful" presents like trainers and clothes for Jimmy. The boys also had presents from the hospital. Jimmy was given a Dr Who mask and Alby had a radio and an MP3 player. Lisa was amazed that they provided presents for patients' siblings. No one was full of Christmas spirit but cheered up when Jim and Linda arrived. They couldn't stay long as they were having dinner with Linda's mum. People still had lives to get on with but, for the time being, Lisa, Mark and Jimmy's lives were on hold. They would celebrate Christmas properly, with Alby, when he was better.

The hospital provided a Christmas dinner for everybody, free of charge. Meals for non-patients usually had to be bought in the hospital canteen but Christmas was the exception. At 1.00pm Lisa and Jimmy ate their Christmas dinner in the Family Room with Lisa and Ricky, Keller's parents, and Keller's siblings Paige, Maddy and Jake. Mark ate his with Karen, whose son James had whooping cough.

Lisa's sister, Nicky, and her husband, Anth, visited in the afternoon. Nicky had collected Lisa's Christmas order from Marks and Spencer. Most of it was in the freezer but Nicky had brought some desserts to the hospital. Shortly afterwards Pauline and Bernie brought buffet food for tea, which they all shared at 6.00pm with Linda and Jim when they returned in the evening. A family Christmas – of sorts.

Lynne and Charlotte were in Ireland with Mark's parents and Mark's brother Tony, with his partner, David, was in Aylesbury. Mark would have liked them to be at the hospital but arrangements had already been made. They would make up for it later, Mark was sure. Life had to go on.

26 December 2007

Alby was moved out of ICU and into the neurological ward – Tiger and Parrot. *Great Ormond Street Hospital is a children's hospital after all*, thought Lisa, *so names that would appeal to children are inevitable.* The intensive care unit hadn't been given an attractive name though – it had been called PICU for Paediatric Intensive Care Unit. Perhaps it was because the children in there wouldn't know or care whether or not it had an appealing name. They just needed to live and get better.

Lisa and Mark noticed that the urgency which had surrounded their arrival had subsided. The stream of visitors had dwindled to a steady trickle of family and close friends. Staff came in to change dressings or check one of Alby's monitors but it became clear that they were just keeping Alby stable. No one had suggested anything to try and make him 'better' and Lisa had stopped asking.

Day by day, little by little, the plans for Alby's future care were revealed. Lisa and Mark set no store by the official prognoses. Lisa had seen the pitying looks from the staff – the looks they exchanged between themselves, the looks they gave Lisa and Mark and the way that they looked at Alby's helpless form. Lisa was beginning to learn that if Alby was to have a chance of any sort of recovery she needed to stay strong and help him fight to get better. She would do everything she could to make sure it happened. She had been helping Alby already, by holding his hand, stroking his face, talking to him and playing his favourite songs.

Lisa didn't know how much of what was going on around him was actually registering in Alby's brain but she knew that it mattered. It mattered very much. She knew that there had been many cases where someone coming out of a deep coma later remembered the music that was played to them and the voices of people around them. That's what Lisa wanted for Alby. Technically, he was awake but Lisa was unsure of how much was registering in Alby's mind. Was he conscious – really conscious? Alby wasn't speaking. Lisa presumed that the brain damage had affected his speech. She asked him questions and talked to him constantly but he didn't respond. He looked at her and she looked at him, willing him to respond but he didn't.

Alby's lack of response didn't deter Lisa and Mark – Alby was bombarded with sensory stimulation. The family talked to Alby as if they expected a response from him. "Alby, it's pouring down outside," "Hope you enjoyed your breakfast – it looked more exciting than mine," "Have you had many visitors today?" Alby was treated in exactly the same way as a fully conscious inpatient in hospital might be treated by

35

others. The conversation, the actions and the information were the same – Alby was a patient and even though it was impossible to gauge his level of awareness, everyone hoped that some of the stimuli would reach through a chink in the wall that surrounded his brain.

Alby's head injuries had left him with dysphagia, which meant he could not swallow. At first, attempts were made to insert nutrition tubes into Alby's stomach but due to a severe attack of pancreatitis food couldn't be digested in that way. It was therefore decided that nutrition would be delivered via a nasal jejunal (NJ) tube just below his stomach and a nasogastric (NG) tube, which delivered medication straight into his stomach.

The tubes frequently moved and each time an X-ray was required to determine the position of the tubes. They also became blocked and Lisa soon learned from the nursing staff that the quickest way to clear a blockage was to syringe the tube with Coca Cola. It became easier for Lisa to deal with the blockages herself than to wait for one of the nursing staff to become available.

31 December 2007

New Year's Eve really meant nothing to Alby's family. Celebrating was the last thing they either wanted to or felt like doing. Everyone was focussing on Alby's progress and decisions had to be made regarding the best way of getting nutrition into Alby. Eventually, it was decided that the safest solution was the insertion of a total parental nutrition (TPN) tube but this had to be fitted into a central vein, under general anaesthetic, so Alby was taken to the operating theatre. The TPN bypassed the intestinal tract completely.

2008 was welcomed in over a meal in the hospital restaurant.

January 2008

The first few days of January flowed into each other and no one seemed to notice the usual demarcations of day and night. The routine remained the same – Lisa, Mark, Scott, Jim and Jimmy had become all too familiar with their parts and played them like veteran actors embrace every new role. Linda, Pauline and Bernie also had their parts and executed them as if they'd been born to them. Everyone talked to Alby as if was conscious and could respond. Lisa hoped that at some point he would respond to the incessant chatter – even if only to tell her to give it a rest! Lisa smiled at the thought – if only.

4 January 2008

Lisa had been told that Alby would need rehabilitation. He would have many complex on-going medical and physiotherapy needs and these would be best met at a specialist rehabilitation unit. Therefore Alby had been put on the waiting list for the The Children's Trust, Tadworth – a rehabilitation unit in Surrey. Lisa immediately went onto the internet to see what she could find out about it.

The Children's Trust, Tadworth had originally been part of Great Ormond Street Hospital but had been a separate organisation for 20 years. It was a place for children with acquired brain injury and the website gave details of its School for Profound Education for pupils with serious and multiple learning difficulties. That filled Lisa with dismay but she read that it was also a place that could boast some astounding successes. She learned about one of the children they had helped. Liam had been severely brain injured after being knocked down by a car. He was in a similar position to Alby and Lisa was encouraged by the story of Liam's success in recovering and returning to education – all due to the care and help he received from The Children's Trust. Suddenly, Lisa found new hope and began to pin everything on Alby's transfer to Tadworth. Unfortunately, The Children's Trust not only had a waiting list but Lisa was told that in order to qualify for a place at Alby needed to be in a hospital local to his home. As Great Ormond Street Hospital had done all that was possible, Alby would have to be transferred to King George's Hospital in Ilford. Lisa knew that she would regard this as some sort of medical waiting room until Alby had a place at Tadworth.

Jimmy

Lisa wanted to return as much as possible to normal. Jimmy was still living with Linda and Jim in Hornchurch but he came to the hospital every night. He was still at primary school and his Headteacher allowed him to spend Wednesdays with his big brother. It was essential to keep Jimmy as involved with his family as possible.

Lisa looked forward to seeing him arrive with Mark on a Tuesday evening. Their Wednesday family time was very precious to them all. It felt like something approaching normality, but Jimmy didn't really want that kind of normality – he wanted everything to be as it was before The Accident. People approached him at school and asked him how Alby was getting on. "All right," he said and either walked away, turned away or tried to change the subject. Some of the parents of the other children must have thought he was rude but Jimmy was sure that none of them understood – he just didn't want to be reminded of it all. His world, with his marvellous mum, super stepdad and brilliant brother had been totally wrecked the previous December. He had only been ten and it wasn't until he was older that he realised how he felt. At the time he was angry. He was angry with the world and everyone in it. He was angry with life. He was angry with the way things had changed.

He was also terribly hurt. He felt physical pain every time he thought of what had happened. He was devoted to Alby and looked up to him. Alby was the big brother who was capable and sorted everything out. Alby led and Jimmy followed. Now Alby couldn't lead so who would Jimmy follow? As his brother started to improve Jimmy wondered if Alby would ever lead again.

Once Jimmy had returned to school after the accident Lisa approached the headteacher to ask that he request parents not to approach Jimmy with questions about Alby. Jimmy didn't want to talk about it and that, in itself, alerted Lisa to the fact that he wasn't coping at all well. She knew that people meant well and she was truly grateful for their concern but she had two sons and, although Alby needed much more attention, it didn't mean that she could just ignore the effect that everything had had on Jimmy.

Alby with his brother Jimmy

9 January 2008

"They have a bed for Alby at King George's, so he will be transferred on Friday," said the consultant, "so I think it's time to say goodbye." Lisa looked round the room and took stock of the situation. She hadn't realised until then that they'd slipped into a routine, much the same as they had had routines at home. Then it had been a normal family routine but this routine was a different family routine, which revolved around the care and attention needed by one very special person. They had established their own routine, caring for and just being with Alby.

It dawned on Lisa that she would miss Great Ormond Street and the friends she had made – both staff and patients. She would miss the friendly banter, the tears and even the laughs. They had made each other laugh over the silliest things but it showed that life was still a curious mixture of ups

39

and downs, sadness and happiness, tears of anguish and tears of joy. It had helped. Suddenly, she panicked. She didn't want to leave Great Ormond Street! Before she knew what was happening, she was in tears and begging the consultant not to make them move. She thought afterwards that it could have been the fear of yet another major upheaval in their lives, one which she felt she couldn't face. "You can stay for the weekend," she was told.

15 January 2008

Alby was transferred to King George's Hospital, Ilford. He went in an ambulance and he went with Lisa and Mark. They went with a curious mixture of apprehension, hope and dread.

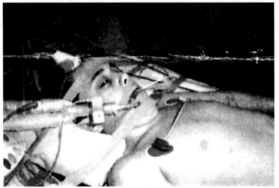

Alby in a critical condition in Great Ormond Street Hospital

Chapter 3
King George's Hospital, Ilford

15 January 2008

Arrival at King George's presented Lisa and Mark with a much more significant change than either of them anticipated. From the moment they arrived it was clear that no one intended that Alby should be 'treated' in the medical sense of the word. Members of staff were pleasant enough but the major part of Alby's day to day care was left to Lisa.

There was no fan to keep Alby cool and there were no bed-sides to keep him safe. There seemed never to be anyone available to change Alby's pads, so Lisa changed them herself rather than let him become uncomfortable. The sites on his legs, where the pins protruded, needed regular and thorough cleaning and this also fell to Lisa.

There was no medical reason why Alby shouldn't be moved but this would have to be done using a wheelchair with a head support and there just wasn't one available. To a certain extent wheelchairs could be adapted to a patient's size and requirements and Alby was measured for this on 21 January. During the five weeks before the wheelchair arrived Alby had to remain in bed, a situation which Lisa and Mark felt was unacceptable but they were powerless to do anything. On 26 February, the wheelchair was finally delivered but it was far too small. Even to an onlooker it seemed to be very uncomfortable for Alby – but he couldn't tell anyone how it felt.

Alby's physiotherapy began but, owing to the size of the room in which Alby was placed, Lisa and Mark had to leave when Alby had his sessions. Lisa was glad to see that something positive was happening. Unfortunately, one day, after the physiotherapists had left, Lisa and Mark went back into the room and discovered that Alby's feeding tube had been left around his neck. Mark swiftly lifted the tube away, grateful that nothing serious had happened. They both realised just how vulnerable Alby was and just how easily a crisis could turn into a disaster.

Mark

Lisa didn't like to cause a fuss and Mark said he would "just have a word with someone" but his anger turned to fury the more he thought about the possible outcome of such a negligent act.

He left the room and as he walked down the corridor he realised he was walking behind the physiotherapists responsible for the situation. Verbally, Mark gave them both barrels.

"What would have happened if Lisa and I hadn't walked in?" he demanded of them. "This is *serious!*" They assured Mark that it wouldn't happen again. "If it happens again there may not be a chance for a anyone to put it right. Don't you people realise how dependent Alby is on your care? Don't you realise that such a stupid, idiotic mistake could have cost him his life? He has come through the most horrific accident and survived and then you lot could have killed him with one thoughtless action!"

Mark was shaking with frustration. How dare they be so calm when he was so upset! He wanted them to feel as upset as he but he knew he couldn't expect them to shout back at him or even to look angry. They looked concerned but that wasn't enough for Mark. Weeks of worry and frustration were taking their toll and deep down Mark knew that he had found a way to vent his feelings, safe in the knowledge that at least he had a genuine reason for his behaviour.

Lisa

Alby's right foot needed to be kept in a plaster cast to keep it at a 90 degree angle to his leg. It kept falling forward and, without intervention, would have healed itself into a horizontal line with his leg. Once a week and usually on a Wednesday, Graham, a plaster technician, gently removed the cast, checked Alby's foot and ankle for sores, and then recast it. Lisa knew that Alby would not be able to walk again without this intervention, and she never gave up hope that he would walk again, one day.

Lisa was amazed that it was possible to perform tests that, in her experience, required communication. But Alby's hearing and eyesight were tested without his apparent input and found to be unaffected by the accident. For that, Lisa was eternally grateful. It meant that there were two hurdles that Alby wouldn't have to conquer.

After a week Alby was moved into a larger room. Bit by bit, little touches of home crept into the room. Lisa had a bed next to Alby and it wasn't long before she brought in matching bed linen for the pair of them. Lisa's determination to bring as much normality as possible into Alby's fragile life knew no bounds! A much-needed kettle soon appeared, followed by a mini-fridge and a clothes rail.

No one knew for how long Alby would be in King George's and they quickly settled into a routine. Mark stayed overnight with Alby on Wednesday and Friday. Lisa stayed on Sunday, Monday, Tuesday, and Thursday. Scott agreed to stay on Saturdays so that Lisa, Mark and Jimmy could have some family time away from the hospital. Lisa and Mark realised that this arrangement would only work if Scott put in an appearance each Saturday. If Scott couldn't make it, Jim stayed at the hospital. It was difficult to have a routine, involving so many people and so much meticulous planning. The failure of just one cog meant that the whole machine malfunctioned so they had to make a change. In March, it was agreed that Scott would take Jimmy to football training on a Friday, after which the two of them would have dinner with Pauline and Bernie. Scott and Jimmy would then return to the hospital where Scott stayed overnight. Lisa, Mark and Jimmy were then able to leave Alby's bedside for their family time, with Lisa and Mark returning at 8am the next morning to continue their cycle of devotion at Alby's bedside.

Mark

Mark often stayed the night to give Lisa time to spend with Jimmy. His first thought on waking was to see that Alby was as comfortable as possible. As Mark approached Alby's bed he noticed that Alby was not in the same position as when Mark had settled down to sleep. Alby was much further towards the edge of the bed and Mark knew that unless some miracle had happened in the night Alby would not have been able to move himself. When he moved Alby's bedclothes he was filled with anger. Alby's bed linen was soaking wet. Alby couldn't help it – it was part of his condition – but someone had been in during the night. Rather than change the bedding they had merely moved Alby to avoid the worst of the dampness. Mark was fired with rage that someone could have treated Alby's vulnerability and dependence on others with such contempt. He stormed out of the room to vent his anger on the senior nurse who'd been in charge overnight. "He must have moved in the night," she said.

"You know full well he can't move! Someone came in and moved him, rather than change his bedding. It's completely unacceptable and I want to know who did this."

The senior nurse hadn't moved Alby herself but she was responsible for the nurse who had. Later that morning the matron came into the room and spoke to Mark, fully supportive of him and after that the nurse who had been responsible for moving Alby never came near him again.

He reflected on the incidents at King George's and regretted that he'd had to complain. When someone is receiving 24 hour care there's a great deal to do and for most of the time Alby's care was what it should have been. He realised that at Great Ormond Street Hospital the staff patient ratio was much lower than it was at King George's and that affects care. Mark felt that the transfer to King George's had been something of a rude awakening. However, Alby's family developed a good relationship with the staff and the majority of them showed compassion and a caring professional attitude towards Alby. Lisa and Mark were on hand most of the time, happy to take over general caring duties and even the administration of Alby's medication. However, Lisa drew a line when she was invited to look at a calculator chart to work out how much medication Alby should have with a view to preparing his medication herself. That was far too much responsibility for someone as emotionally fragile as she knew herself to be and the thought of getting it wrong terrified her. She refused.

Jim

Alby had problems that presented Grandad Jim with opportunities to help. Alby had contracted an infection around the site of the pins in his leg and he had to be given intravenous antibiotics. With painstaking care and the gentlest of touches, Jim cleaned the wounds around the pins in his grandson's legs. It was the least he could do.

Alby needed to be fed water and Jim jumped at the chance to do this for his grandson. He gently dripped water into Alby's parched mouth and then, even more gently, he massaged the throat he was trying to coax into life. Day after day Jim persevered. Sometimes Alby's lips seemed so dry Jim thought they would shatter and he was reluctant to risk making them sore by even gently prising them apart in his efforts to help Alby relearn such a basic reflex. Jim's efforts were tireless and one day, in early March, Alby swallowed. It happened quietly but Alby's family wanted to shout it from the top of the hospital building. He could now begin eating again.

Lisa and Mark

It seemed such a simple thing but it was a major breakthrough. Alby could swallow. This simple ability had far-reaching effects for Alby's family. Alby no longer needed a feeding tube and, to everyone's delight, he would be allowed home visits. Lisa and Mark couldn't wait to take him there, to welcome him and to have just one little thing that resembled a normal life again. They knew it would be difficult with Alby's wheelchair but they regarded this as a small price to pay for the happiness they felt and the happiness they anticipated.

16 March 2008

Alby's first day home! Jim had stayed at the hospital overnight and travelled with everyone when Alby came home in an ambulance. Alby was completely reliant on his wheelchair and could only travel in a suitable vehicle. The whole family was waiting for his arrival. This day was important and marked the first stage in what everyone hope would be Alby's return to his old life. Everyone hoped silently, everyone prayed silently but no one wanted to say anything. They all felt it might break the spell of Alby's recovery if they articulated their thoughts.

Everyone was choked with emotion, some speechless with delight, when Alby was brought into the living room he'd left three months earlier. The smiles, the hugs and the tears were overwhelming.

Lisa thought she would never forget that very important first meal at home. Alby ate mashed potatoes and gravy.

23 March 2008

It may have been Easter Sunday, but Alby and his family hadn't had their Christmas dinner at home, so that is what they all enjoyed on Alby's second visit home. The Christmas fare that had been so hastily put into the freezer, wasn't the only thing frozen. Time had been frozen. It seemed that everyone was bursting with belated Christmas cheer. No one needed to be told but they were all mindful of so much more than material blessings. Alby was alive. Alby was getting better. Alby was home. Christmas had come.

6 May 2008

The consultant smiled at Lisa as he delivered the news. "A place for Alby has become available at The Children's Trust and, if it's OK with you, Mum, he will be transferring there next week."

Lisa jumped up from her chair, threw her arms around the consultant and hugged him so hard he nearly toppled over. After four months at Ilford, Lisa was given the news for which she had been waiting – Alby was going to Tadworth! She was overjoyed. She had known that King George's was only a stop gap and she knew that it wouldn't be until he went to Tadworth that he was likely to make any significant progress. It wasn't that the staff at King George's hadn't done their best because they had, but Tadworth was more specialised in dealing with cases like Alby's.

Lisa roped everyone into helping her prepare for Alby's move. Alby's name would have to be sewn into every item of clothing he had, so all visitors – friends or family – were given labels, a needle and thread. Some of them, particularly some of the men, had never sewn anything in their lives but Lisa's enthusiasm made everyone want to pitch in. There was a very distinct party atmosphere in Alby's room that week and Lisa was kept busy packing all their belongings. Get well cards covered an entire wall and during Alby's stay much of their home had found its way into to his room – bed linen, kettle, mini-fridge – and it all had to be packed up for the move.

Although Lisa was more excited about the move than she could say, she had made friends with the staff at King George's and there were tears and hugs as the family said their goodbyes. Lisa had always been the type of person to make the best of any situation and people warmed to her openness and grounded approach to the one in which she and her family found themselves.

When everything had been removed, Lisa took one last look at the room. It was bare and looked bleak and uninviting. Lisa shrugged her shoulders. It had been their home from home but now they were off on a new adventure. As long as they were all together they could make a home anywhere.

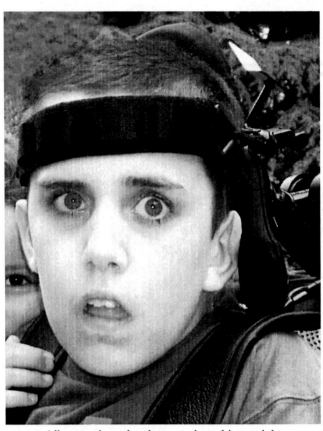

Alby wearing a head cage to keep him upright

Chapter 4
The Children's Trust, Tadworth

13 May 2008

The ambulance engine hummed, singing a mechanical lullaby. Lisa was buoyed with excitement but tired. Tired from the months of anguish that had gnawed away at her, exposing emotions she didn't know existed. She allowed her thoughts free rein. This was T-day. Lisa named this day T-day because it would be Alby's final push to get better at Tadworth. Well, just for now, to be better than he was. Alby's family didn't know where his rehabilitation at The Children's Trust would lead them or him but they had faith. It may have been blind faith but it was faith and they had it by the bucketful. Lisa pressed her face to the car window, like a child eager for their first glimpse of the sea. What she saw surprised her. The landscape was filled with a magnificent old country house standing behind lawns cascading to two levels and surrounded by carefully sculpted shrub beds. "Wow," she turned to look at the driver. "Have you got the right place? This doesn't look like a hospital." The driver smiled. "I think we'll move in – it looks great. Alby, d'you fancy moving in here? Well, guess what, I can grant your wish." Lisa laughed and looked at Alby for a reaction that never came. He was a good boy. He always had been. They were taking him to Tadworth and he just sat there and let them. Lisa wiped a tear from the corner of her eye, telling herself that it was early days and, for goodness sake, they'd only just arrived.

Mark followed in the car. He knew what to expect as he'd researched The Children's Trust on the internet. He also knew that as far as specialism was concerned it didn't come any better than this place. Mark understood the function of the place that was to be Alby's last chance and he made sure he knew exactly what Alby was likely to experience when he became one of their learners.

Leaving the M25 at any point, for any reason, is always a joy for the one turning their back on what may well have been one of the most stressful modern road journeys ever encountered. Yet, close to this concrete snake, slithering through the soft lushness of Surrey's countryside, is an oasis of calm, encouragement and hope. Just as one brings out the very worst in human nature, so the other brings out the very best.

Describing itself as a 'national charity working with children with acquired brain injury, multiple disabilities and complex health needs' The Children's Trust greets its visitors with a foliage-lined driveway which leads to a 17th-century manor house. It was built around 1694, after the estate was bought by Leonard Wessel, a merchant. Pevsner, chronicler of fine English buildings, described Tadworth Court as a 'splendid house' and 'one of the most elegant in the whole country.' The 24 acre site was eventually bought by Great Ormond Street Hospital for Sick Children in 1927 and from 1929 was used as their convalescent 'outpost' to give children recovering from lung conditions, such as tuberculosis, a chance to recuperate. It was felt that after breathing in the soot and grime with which London air was laden, the clean air of the Surrey countryside would be beneficial.

In the early 1980s the Department for Health decided to sell Tadworth Court. Mr Tim Yeo, Member of Parliament, backed by The Sun newspaper, spearheaded a campaign to save it and in 1983 it became separate from Great Ormond Street to operate as an independent body. The Children's Trust, although working as a charitable trust, continued to take patients from Great Ormond Street, although the profile of those using the services of the Trust changed. In 1985 it became the UK's first dedicated brain injury unit for children and it remains the largest. Now, the Trust's client base consists of children with profound and multiple learning difficulties and complex health needs as well as those with acquired brain injuries.

The Trust provides residential care for some children who only go home on alternate weekends. Other students go home each day but for every student, residential or day, everything is geared to the child's needs. Just as there would have been in 1929, routines exist, but nursing care and rehabilitation is tailored to the individual.

The Trust also teaches parents so that, if possible, they are in a position to care for their child at home. In the past, it was rarely possible for the parents of a sick or injured child to stay at the hospital. If exceptional circumstances permitted it, the best a parent could hope for would be a camp bed beside their child's hospital bed. Now, parents have their own accommodation and can be there, beside their child, the nursing staff and therapists, all the time.

The reception area is to the right of the entrance. Visitors are greeted by wood panelled arches and, although architecturally very imposing, there is nothing intimidating about the atmosphere. From the moment visitors step through the doors they sense warmth and a strong sense of purpose. The gentle hum of those engaged in their daily routine is as reassuring as the smiles.

The grand manor house is now the administrative centre for the Trust with nursing care and rehabilitation taking place in the centres which have been built in the grounds. It is easy to see how the Trust gives 'the best opportunity to make the best recovery'. Walking through the house and its grand rooms, which are now used as a canteen, meetings rooms and offices, the buildings that house the work of The Children's Trust come into view.

They all have names associated with nature – Woodlands, Willow, Chestnut, Jasmine, Cedar, Camelia, Mulberry, Hawthorn, Oak and Maple. The names fit the therapeutic nature of the place – its setting, its aims and the work itself.

The School for Profound Education provides an all-encompassing, varied and rich diet of education and therapies for its learners. Learners are children and young people with physical and cognitive disabilities, who range from 5 to 25 years of age. 19-25 year olds attend the special college. All learners experience a programme of tailor-made activities, which include music therapy, speech and language therapy, hydrotherapy, physiotherapy, occupational therapy and even aromatherapy. A wide range of off-site outings and activities extend the learners' experiences outside of Tadworth Court. One example of this is the link the school has with a local riding school. Art, music, dance and drama form part of the curriculum, just as it would in any other school. Students can even experience 'rebound therapy' on a trampoline, helping their muscle strength, communication and social interaction skills. Specialist equipment is built into the fabric of the classroom and this allows students to be safely lifted and transported. An underfloor tracking system gives students the sensation of travelling unassisted. *Alby is going to love it here*, thought Mark.

The way that staff swung into action when Alby and his entourage arrived at The Children's Trust reminded Lisa of the staff at Queen's Hospital – purposeful, experienced, knowledgeable. They took over and filled Lisa with a new-found confidence for Alby's future. She kept thinking of Tadworth's success stories and convinced herself that Alby would be one of them. No one had told her otherwise. No one would tell her otherwise. After all, who would want to extinguish even the slightest spark of optimism in what had been the black cavern of Lisa's dreads?

The family was initially given two rooms – one for Lisa and Mark; one for Scott and Jimmy. During the first week Lisa, Mark and Scott were immersed in plans for Alby's rehabilitation – and there were many. They attended every meeting, every assessment and every session concerning Alby. They met doctors, nurses and support workers. They listened to the specialists, therapists and professionals who would help rebuild Alby's life. They explored the local area. Lisa, Mark and Jimmy discovered the delights of Tadworth, Sutton and Epsom. They found Chinese and Indian restaurants and takeaways, pizza parlours and burger palaces. There was a restaurant for staff and parents at The Children's Trust but sometimes they went offsite. They found a local supermarket with a restaurant where Lisa often went for a meal with the friends she had made at the Trust. They knew that after two weeks, one of the rooms that they had been given would be withdrawn, and when that happened Scott and Jimmy had to return home. They would then become visitors instead of residents.

Chapter 5
Life at Tadworth

Alby had his first shower in five months. His regime of drugs was arranged. The staff organised his feeding schedule. Lisa stepped back, unsure of how she was feeling. Everything at the Trust seemed to be so positive by comparison with what she and Alby had experienced recently elsewhere. Although Lisa was overjoyed with what was happening she was uneasy and she didn't know why. She realised suddenly that she felt redundant. She had become so used to doing everything for Alby that she found it difficult to stand back and watch others doing it all. *How do I fit in now?* she thought.

Alby's need for specialist equipment to help him with everyday living was addressed – bath equipment, a sling, a hoist, a standing frame and a walking frame. The next day Alby's routine began and Lisa was amazed that so much could be fitted into a day. Alby's 'work' routine, which started at 9.00am, was divided into one-hour sessions, which were a combination of therapies, each lasting half an hour or an hour. First to appear was the physiotherapy team, who immediately organised a suitable wheelchair. Lisa nearly cried with joy when she saw the wheelchair, knowing that it would give Alby freedom. She knew it would be limited freedom but after what had happened over the past few months she also knew that this was a major step forward. This wheelchair was so very different from the one Alby had been given at King George's. It fitted Alby, it had a headrest and it was comfortable. Alby couldn't tell her how it felt, but just as she knew the other one had been uncomfortable, so she knew that this one was perfect.

Alby was measured for a spinal jacket, which would prevent curvature of his spine. A plaster cast of Alby's body was made to ensure the jacket was a perfect fit. When it arrived Lisa thought it looked like something from a Star Wars film. Two solid pieces of blue plastic were fitted over his chest and back and then secured by the three straps on each side. Each day, Alby would don a T-shirt, then the jacket and then another T-shirt or sweater.

Alby was strapped into the new wheelchair. He was supported around his head and his thighs. So began the first of many sessions to help him regain and strengthen his wasted muscles. Physiotherapist Belinda stood behind him and encouraged him into a sitting position. She held him and slowly removed her support, telling Alby that he could do it on his own. Many times he fell sideways, unable to take the weight of his own body, but Belinda wasn't one to give up and neither was Alby. Eventually, he did it. Once he had found his balance, he was encouraged to try and keep his legs together instead of letting them flop apart. Lisa watched, waited and wondered. She watched the slow but steady progress that they were making with her son. She waited to see how far they could take him. She wondered if those poor battered legs would ever walk again. She dismissed every hope almost as soon as it sprang into her head, just grateful for the progress that the day had brought.

Alby was encouraged to use his arms as much as possible. Gently, his arms were persuaded to move upwards, outwards and in front of him. His right arm was much more receptive to this persuasion than his left. No one was sure whether Alby understood the ceaseless encouragement he was given, but it never faltered. "Come on, Alby, you can do it! There, look, you've done it! Just a little bit more now…" and so it continued.

No one waited for Alby to clear one hurdle before presenting him with the next challenge – and challenges came fast and furious at Tadworth. New skills had to be learnt and the physio teams saw to it that he didn't rest on his laurels. He was shown how to wash and dress himself and although he still needed a great deal of help, he quickly learnt to manage small tasks unaided.

Physiotherapy sessions were relentless. Therapy is a word that Lisa associated with gentle persuasion but it seemed that the sessions through which Alby battled every day were anything but gentle. Twisting and turning his arms and legs, determination gripped his whole body as he pushed and pushed at the boundaries that restricted his movement. Day by day, hour by hour, bit by bit he heaved his effort against the hand that fate had dealt him and that effort eventually turned the tide of his restricted movements. Inch by inch, Alby was moving forward in more ways than one. Over fourteen months many of these sessions were recorded. Lisa would watch them months later and be constantly in awe of her son's progress.

Increased confidence with sitting lead to Alby's next major challenge – standing. At first he stood with support – straps, a frame and a huge amount of willpower. Alby wasn't speaking but determination was written all over his face. Encouraged by the staff, Lisa and Mark, Alby's body frequently shook with the sheer effort of supporting his emaciated frame. At first his legs were guided, slowly and carefully, by skilled hands, but gradually he made small movements on his own. Gripping the frame as if he was on a roller coaster, Alby dragged one foot along the floor and staff helped him to position it correctly. He was frequently exhausted and staff wondered from where he found more energy, but find it he did and with almost superhuman effort he then slowly dragged the other foot forward.

The occupational therapists designed sessions to improve Alby's fine motor skills. He only had the use of one hand and the extraordinary effort required for even the smallest gesture made Alby exceptionally tired. Sometimes he would fall asleep during the session and Camilla (known as 'Milla) very gently rubbed an ice ball over his face to wake him and keep him focussed. *That was just like him falling asleep over his dinner when he was a baby*, thought Lisa. A simple task, like pressing a button on a computer, was a major hurdle for Alby, but he persevered until he did it.

Pi, the speech and language therapist began visiting Alby daily and later, Sam entered the arena of Alby's therapy. Lisa was grateful for any specialist help given to Alby but wondered why on earth it was felt that speech and language therapy would be of any benefit. Alby had not spoken since the accident. His eyes were open but Lisa did not see him respond to anything around him. She sometimes wondered but at the same time desperately hoped that something of day to day events were filtering through the fog that surrounded Alby's consciousness. She imagined sunlight breaking through early morning mists. At first the sun seems too weak for the task it faces but it keeps burning steadily through the mist and suddenly the mist dissipates, bathing everything in warm sunshine. Lisa wondered if this could possibly happen to Alby. Would the sounds, sights and smells that surrounded him keep burning through? Would he be storing them up? Would he be able to remember them? Would he ever be able to talk about them? Sam had a variety of speech aids to help and encourage Alby – a computer that replicated noises and vowel sounds.

Sam encouraged Alby with his eating skills. Regaining his swallowing reflex just before he left King George's meant that he was only given milk feeds, via a tube, for a very short time before he was introduced to soft foods. The staff at Tadworth checked that the food Alby was swallowing was following the right path. His external muscles had taken a huge battering and no one knew what might have happened to those muscles responsible for pushing food through his gut. Adding barium to Alby's food enabled its progress to be monitored through a video capsule endoscopy and everyone was delighted to find that everything was OK. He could now eat normally. No more feeding tubes. Staring at the mashed potato, gravy and finely chopped vegetables, Lisa thought back to Alby's first efforts to eat solid food and realised that he was just like that baby again – except this time he was learning everything for the second time. Lisa noticed that the speech and language therapy focus was on Alby's eating skills as he still wasn't speaking. Swallowing was a new skill for Alby and eating food slowly was as much as he could manage but fluids still had to be administered via a tube.

At midday, Alby joined five other children for lunch. Alby, Ahmed and Shanice were able to eat but the others had to be fed via a tube. Eating was a step in the right direction. When the children had finished their lunch they rested before sessions resumed at 2pm, finishing at 4pm. Alby was exhausted by this new regime. By comparison with what he had experienced since his accident, the activities were physically and mentally pushing him to his absolute limit. When everyone thought he had reached that limit, they pushed him to find a new one. By 6pm he could barely keep his eyes open but going to bed at such an early hour had a downside – Alby was awake and raring to go again at three or four o'clock in the morning! Lisa was relieved when Alby's bedtime gradually moved to eight or nine o'clock as he grew stronger and more used to the routine.

Once he was eating normally, Alby's speech and language therapy concentrated on communication. As he couldn't speak, he would learn to communicate by other means. He worked with picture recognition and pushing buttons on a computer. It didn't matter whether it was to make someone aware of his needs or whether it was just to have a conversation, at least he was communicating.

Lisa continued with her apparently ceaseless optimism, especially in front of Alby, but she found weekends difficult. Although she hadn't particularly warmed to King George's the hospital had been close to the amenities. She was within walking distance of shops and therefore a break from the claustrophobic atmosphere in the hospital. She neither needed nor wanted a break from her son, but the hospital – well, that was a different matter. Tadworth Court was not close to any amenities. In fact, it was not close to anywhere! The intensity of the weekday routine suddenly stopped on Friday afternoons. The sounds generated by machines, human conversation, laughter and tears evaporated as though spirited away to another dimension. The silence didn't last for long. Mark, Jimmy, Pauline, Bernie, Linda, Jim and Lisa's sisters visited at weekends. Lisa thought it was as though her family had moved in. The noise, the laughter and the closeness made her feel more at home than she would have thought possible. There was only one thing missing – Alby's dog, Honey. With some trepidation, Lisa asked the staff if Honey would be allowed to visit. She was unsure. After all, it wasn't a hospital in the conventional sense of the word, so she felt it was worth a try. She was told that it was a brilliant idea and having Honey around might help Alby with his recovery. A very excited and overjoyed Honey left no one in any doubt about who was the centre of her universe. Alby looked at her and Lisa knew right away that she had been right to ask. Something in Alby's eyes told her that he had recognised the little white bundle dancing up and down on her back legs, her black eyes radiating love for her playmate.

Parents like Lisa and Mark lived in the old Nurses Home and the children lived in Hawthorn House. On Tuesday, Mark brought Jimmy to Tadworth. He slept on a camp bed between Lisa and Mark's beds. He stayed Tuesday night and went back with Mark and Lisa on Wednesday for family time. They sometimes went to the cinema. Sometimes they just stayed at home with a pizza and watched TV. It was very important that Jimmy had some semblance of a normal family life. Jim went every Thursday and stayed until Lisa returned. This arrangement continued until September, when Jimmy started attending his new secondary school. Pauline also came to Tadworth on Tuesdays, which was family visiting day. She often accompanied Alby to his half hour physio and occupational therapy sessions, each morning and afternoon.

They formed friendships with the other adults – there is something about common adversity that binds people together. People who perhaps might never even have met, let alone become friends in any other situation, suddenly forged bonds through their shared anxiety for their children. They met Sharma, whose mum stayed with her and whose dad stayed in one of the flats. They met Ahmed whose dad had the

59

second flat. They met Mohammed whose mum moved into a flat when Sharma's family left.

They had all been at the Trust longer than Lisa and had meshed together, forming their own invisible club. They were very kind to her but Lisa always thought of herself as the new girl and she felt as if she was intruding. Initially there had been a great deal to do, but once Alby's routine was established, Mark had to return to work and Jimmy had to return to school. Lisa was finding her existence in Hawthorn House quite lonely. She often stayed with Alby until he fell asleep. Then she would watch TV and DVDs in her room. When another new girl arrived, she and Lisa formed an immediate friendship. Claire and her daughter had been at the Trust before so Claire knew the ropes. This meant that she wasn't really a new girl. She could see that Lisa was feeling isolated and it was obvious after their first conversation that they would get on really well.

April 2008

Mark

"You've never been sporty," said Lisa.

"I know but I…" hesitated Mark.

"Did you like sport at school?"

"Well, not really but I suppose I didn't really mind cross country."

"So, you didn't really do sport but you liked cross country a bit, and now you want to run the London Marathon of all things! Mark, it's 26 miles and you only ever run to catch a bus! You're completely off your trolley!" She shook her head in exasperation but laughing gently as she poured scorn on Mark's very genuine expression of philanthropy.

Mark had a Bucket List – things he wanted to do before it was too late. One of those things was to run the London Marathon. Mark wasn't sporty and had never really run, other than in compulsory cross country sessions at school or perhaps to catch a bus – as Lisa had pointed out. He didn't even know why he found the prospect of running 26.2 miles (to be precise) so appealing. Mark thought it was probably fate that The Children's Trust was the nominated charity for the London Marathon the following year and he took it as a sign that he should go for it. So, in the early summer of 2008 Mark began his regime of running. Laps around the grounds of Tadworth Court and the village became a common occurrence and people became used to seeing Mark, clad in only shorts and a vest, pounding his way over the frost encrusted grass. He sometimes questioned his own sanity for starting this venture but he was so grateful for what The Children's Trust was doing for Alby that he couldn't give up. He owed them something and this was his way of giving back. He might not be able to manage it but he knew he would give it his best shot. He also knew he would need a great deal of practise and that practise gave him plenty of time to think.

September 2004

"To bowl or not to bowl, that is the question." Well, at least it was the question that faced Mark. "It'll be great fun, you'll really enjoy it and anyway, give me one reason why you wouldn't want to spend a brilliant evening with me and Steve?" laughed Jo. Like so many of his friends, Steve and Jo meant well. Mark was 'nisi'd,' as he liked to think of it. Not married, not divorced but lurking in that sort of twilight zone where divorcees find themselves in the interim before some faceless Judge, who has never met them and probably couldn't care less about their tragic story, puts the final stamp on the official End of the Marriage – the Decree Absolute.

Jo was still talking. "…and so Sharon, this friend of ours I told you about – oh Mark, don't look like that! I *know* I told you about her. Anyway," she continued, taking a deep breath, clearly in readiness for a verbal onslaught that would brook no interruption, "Sharon has this friend called Lisa and she's in the same position as you and no, we are not trying to match-make before you say anything, but she is coming along too because Sharon's her friend and obviously Sharon wants her friends at her party. So, are you coming?"

Mark thought that if talking was an Olympic sport, she could win gold, and he didn't want to seem ungrateful but…

Oh my goodness, he thought, *did I just think ungrateful? Am I already such a sad case that I have to feel grateful for any crumbs of female contact my friends throw me?* Mark wondered if he should also be grateful for their friendship too. Jo and Steve had been friends with him and his soon-to-be-ex-wife and, following The Split had decided to stay friends with Mark. He decided that he was grateful, at least for the friendship, after all.

Mark was quite content, thank you. It's a pity that his friends couldn't see it but after two years of being at the receiving end of the bickering chisel which had chipped away not only at his confidence but also his hopes of a happy marriage, he wanted peace. *Forget happy*, he thought, *and give me peace any day!* His wife, (and *yes* he reminded himself, *she still was his wife, for now at any rate*) seemed like a complete stranger. Meeting, marriage and misery. In that order. Looking back, he realised how incompatible they really were but it had taken two years to realise that his 13 year old marriage was never going to work.

Friends are great – generally. The main problem with friends was that they look at you and see what they want to see. Like most men, Mark hadn't said too much when his marriage was disintegrating, because he was a man and real men don't do 'soft' but inside he was feeling like the biggest failure in the universe. As soon as Judge Faceless had done the decent thing and in effect given him permission to start a new life he was off to Ireland. As an Assistant Store Manager for Next he thought his job prospects would be good more or less anywhere in the British Isles, so to County Cork it was! It made him feel like an intrepid adventurer but the truth was that his parents lived there.

Lisa

Lisa had lost her zest for marriage but not her zest for life or having fun. Six years of Scott had given her a marriage, a lovely home, two gorgeous sons and the nightmare of wondering where her husband had disappeared to for days at a time. Divorce was inevitable and Lisa was contemplating singledom much as one would view a trip to the supermarket – not really exciting but has to be done for survival.

"It's only my birthday, after all," said Sharon "so yes, you do have to come along – and you might meet a man there. OK, he might look like Shrek but you might get on and then you can invite him to the Christmas party. It'd save you going on your own and being Billy-No-Mates all evening!"

Mark

October 2004 and Bowling Evening arrived. Mark told himself that this friend of Sharon's, Lisa, probably had a very pleasant personality but she could well have been a winner at Crufts and that wouldn't disappoint him because he wasn't interested. He'd told Jo and Steve that he wasn't interested. All he was interested in was having a reasonably enjoyable night out and of course he would be polite to Lisa because that's the decent sort of chap he was, he told himself.

He heard her laughter before he saw her. It was the sort of laugh that made you smile even though you didn't know what or who was the cause of it. It was infectious and Mark thought it was a really stupid way of describing really genuine laughter. "Someone's found something *really* funny," he mused.

A pair of blue eyes suddenly turned their beam in his direction. *No Crufts there then,* thought Mark. *This is going to be awkward. She's attractive. No, not just attractive – very attractive – and I don't want to be attracted to her. I am fine on my own and I just can't do all that relationship stuff again. It's far too soon to even think about it.* At first Mark was relieved that they were bowling in separate lanes, but every time it was his turn to assume the position at the end of the lane, it seemed to be Lisa's turn too. They tried not to look at each other but each time Mark looked up, he found himself staring into Lisa's 'rather interesting' eyes (Mark groaned inwardly at his own cliché thought) and every time Lisa looked up Mark seemed to be smiling at her.

Unfortunately for Mark's determination, he and Lisa got on very well. They had a similar sense of humour and laughed at the same ridiculous things. Mark found Lisa easy to talk to. If anything, he considered himself towards the upper end of the Shy Scale, but Lisa would have put anyone at their ease. At the end of the evening Mark said his goodbyes and left.

Lisa

Sharon dug Lisa in the ribs. "Who's got herself a new man then?"

"Oh for goodness' sake!" Lisa snapped but, at the same time, couldn't help grinning. "He's just a nice person…to talk to…as a friend."

"A friend who would possibly be good company for you at the Christmas party…"

"Maybe," said Lisa hesitantly.

"In that case lady, I suggest you get out into that car park pretty sharpish before he leaves and ask him to that party, *as a friend*," Sharon added sarcastically. She glared at Lisa and laughed.

"And that's wrong because…?" questioned Lisa.

"For crying out loud, go and ask him before he disappears, you idiot."

Lisa and Mark

Lisa tore out of the building and was just in time. Mark was in the car and ready to start the engine when he saw her running across the car park. He wound down the window, already pleased to see her again. There was no gremlin on his shoulder telling him to slow down as he beamed at Lisa.

"Look," she gasped "I know we've only just met but there's this Christmas party and I'm single and you're single and I thought that perhaps, it might be an idea, only if you're free…"

"I'd love to go with you," Mark replied and they exchanged phone numbers. Lisa turned to walk away but Mark called her back. "If we're going to this 'do' together, we might as well get to know each other, so what do you say to meeting up next week?"

Lisa said 'yes' to meeting up next week and the venue was a Doubles Bar in Canary Wharf, near to Lisa's workplace. Their next date was for a Chinese meal. Mark knew that Lisa came as a one third part of a package of three, so after that they took her sons, 10-year-old Alby and eight-year-old Jimmy, to the cinema. Mark joined Lisa and the boys for Christmas dinner. They talked on the phone every night, sometimes for three or four hours.

The 'Absolutes' from their respective divorces came through. In July 2005 they became engaged. In July 2006 they were married.

Scott continued to see the boys, usually at his parents' house, but Lisa had no further contact with him. It wasn't necessary.

June 2008

Lisa's friends Mimi and Glen were visiting Alby. Lisa was constantly trying to stimulate Alby's thoughts and she asked him where each of his visitors were. Each time Alby's eyes moved to look at the person. That was progress. Lisa was impatient for more but she knew that if there was to be more it would happen when Alby was ready and not because she was wishing for it.

July 2008

Lisa

In early July Sally arrived with her daughter, Danielle. Sally occupied the room opposite Lisa in the nurses' home. The two women hit it off immediately. Sally and Lisa met outside the building, both feeling guilty that they were smokers. They laughed as they looked at each other conspiratorially, both outcast by their habit. They spent many hours together, sometimes talking, sometimes laughing and sometimes crying. Often they were still putting the world to rights at 4am but it was July and it was warm, so they didn't really notice the hour. Sally stayed at Tadworth for four months and she and Lisa were grateful for the unspoken support and friendship of the other.

Alby continued to make good progress with his therapies and Lisa continued with her never-ending chat. She didn't know how much of what she said had got through to Alby but she had begun to suspect that it was a worthwhile exercise. Lisa's friend Meme and her husband Glen visited and, like all visitors, coaxed, cajoled and encouraged Alby as much as they could. "Look Alby," and his eyes would move. "Do you like my new top?" "Phew, it's warm today." "Here's Glen, come to see you fella!" He began responding to questions about objects by moving his eyes. "Alby, where's the window? Where are your trainers? Where's grandad?" Lisa was overjoyed and wondered whether the sun had started burning through that mist. She watched, waited and hoped. She knew that Alby could see everything and she was comforted by the fact that his eyesight and hearing were unaffected by the accident. People spoke. Alby looked. But that was it. Well, it was until Jimmy opened his laptop computer and found some films of footballers who had been tackled in amusing ways. Lisa watched Jimmy roaring with laughter and she turned to Alby, who was also watching the footage. She caught her breath as she looked at him – he was smiling. For the first time since December, Alby was smiling. Lisa clapped her hands and ran to Alby. "Jimmy! Jimmy! Alby is smiling!" she shrieked.

Jimmy turned to his brother and hugged him. "OK fella?" he said. "Nice one."

Home

July was also the month when Alby was allowed home for a whole weekend and during his first visit home to Harold Wood he was accompanied by 'Milla. She wanted to see how Alby would get on and how his family would cope with his additional needs. She needed to check wheelchair accessibility and the position regarding the addition of a bath sling and hoist. The family knew that they would have to adapt their home to accommodate Alby when he left

Tadworth Court. Mark drove Alby home in a van. It would have been impossible to get all the equipment Alby needed – the wheelchair, the hoist, the frames – into a car.

This was their first opportunity, as a family together, to open the Christmas presents that had remained wrapped and pitifully untouched since Alby's accident. Alby and Jimmy had been given a TV for their bedroom but Alby would have to have his own room. Bernie's' sister, Audrey, had given them money and asked them to use it to buy whatever was needed, so they decided to use it for a TV for Alby's room. Scott had given Alby a Play Station, which he took back to Tadworth Court with him.

In late July Mark's parents, Nora and Tom came over from Ireland. They were Alby's third set of grandparents and Alby liked them. They sat with him for several hours, chatting about their home, their journey, what they'd been doing in Ireland and what they planned doing during their stay. "Once you get out of here we'll get Mark to bring you all over for a visit. Give us a chance to spoil you rotten!" Nora and Tom, like everyone else, talked to Alby as if it was part of a normal, two way conversation. They left at five o'clock.

Mark

It was late afternoon and still a beautiful day. The sun was shining and a warm breeze was blowing through the open windows into Alby's room. The smell of the freshly cut grass wafted through the windows, dispensing its summery scent to all in its path. Mark thought about his parents, Nora and Tom, who had been to see Alby. It was too good a running day to waste so Mark suddenly announced that he was going for a run. By now, his shorts and vest top didn't look so incongruous with the weather. He did his usual laps of the grounds thinking of how his performance was gradually improving but still sometimes wondering at his decision. Was it really reckless? He was a novice and he knew there would be seasoned runners taking part. However, Mark didn't look on the London Marathon as a competition. He didn't even want to beat anyone. He just wanted to complete the course in his best possible time, raising as much money as he could.

Lisa

Lisa returned to her position at Alby's side. "Well, Alby, what a lovely afternoon you've had. I see you've had more visitors. Who's been to see you then?" She started to turn away but then froze when she heard the answer. Slowly, but clearly, she heard Alby's response.

"T-o-m." It was slow but it was definitely 'Tom'. Time stopped. Lisa felt pole-axed. The shock hit her with the force of a hammer. She reeled. "What did you say?" she shrieked, she grinned, she gasped! Alby looked at her.

"T-o-m."

Lisa threw herself on him and hugged him. She was in shock but delighted. "Oh my goodness! Can you say love you?" Alby said it. "Sam! Sam! Come in here! Quick! Alby spoke! Listen!" Sam, a nurse, was on duty and heard Lisa's cries. She tore through the door, not knowing why Lisa was screaming so loudly and fearing the worst. By this time Lisa was crying. Through the sobs she managed to tell Sam what had happened and begged her to listen. Alby repeated himself and within minutes the room was crowded with people wanting to share this very special moment. Doctors, nurses, cleaners, other parents – they all wanted to share the joy.

Mark

The sun was burning the back of his neck and he was glad to arrive back at Hawthorn House, breathless and hot but feeling very positive about his progress. He pushed the doors and heard the commotion long before he saw it. It was excitement as Mark had never seen it before. Elation was everywhere. People were smiling, crying, exclaiming, "Oh my goodness; it's wonderful; how brilliant; amazing," and as he cautiously approached Alby's room Mark could see that therein was the source.

Lisa's tear-streaked face turned towards him. "Oh Mark," sobbed Lisa as she looked at her husband framed in the doorway. "Oh Mark! Listen to Alby." Alby looked towards Mark and said,

"Mark."

Lisa asked Alby the sixty-four-thousand-dollar question again and Alby slowly replied, "T-o-m." He was grinning. Mark thought his heart would burst and it had nothing to do with the running.

Alby

"Alby, what's this?"

"Trainer."

"What colour is it?"

"White."

The room became more and more crowded. People were hugging Lisa and each other. Lisa looked at Alby in amazement. She hugged him time and time again, encouraging him to identify more objects.

From then on there was no stopping him. Over the course of the next few days all areas of Alby's memory were tested. He was counting to ten in French. He was completing some simple mental arithmetic calculations. Before his accident he'd been well versed in his times tables and Alby soon proved that his ability to recall them was unaffected.

At last the speech and language therapists had something into which they could sink their professional teeth. Initially, Alby was encouraged to enunciate vowels. Then he was encouraged to speak into a microphone, which was connected to a computer and the sounds made by Alby caused an onscreen ball to bounce. Such was the progress he made that Alby was moved from the Orange to the Red teaching room, which was for children with a better level of understanding of their surroundings and improved cognitive abilities.

September 2008

Jimmy started at Shenfield High School – the school that Alby had attended. He stopped visiting Tadworth during the week. Alby was making steady progress and Lisa and Mark wanted Jimmy to resume as normal a life as possible. They felt that starting at his new school would give him that. Jimmy settled into life at Shenfield where many of Alby's friends already knew him, which gave him a very good start. To be known and liked by some of the older boys gave him status with his peers and he was relatively happy. Unfortunately, when staff discovered that Alby's younger brother had started at the school, they naturally asked after Alby and Jimmy felt as if he was re-living the nightmare. Alby was still at Tadworth Court and Jimmy was living with his grandparents. He adored them and was very happy with them but it didn't alter the fact that this horrible thing had happened to his family and it had felt as if he had a knife lodged right inside him. Nothing would shift it now and nothing was likely to shift in in the future. When people kept asking questions, it felt as if it was being wiggled about, just to remind him it was there! Such was his distress that Lisa has to contact the school and ask that no more enquiries be directed at Jimmy. She knew they would understand.

I'm a Celebrity

During his time at The Children's Trust, Alby met many famous people. The work of the organisation attracted the attention of many celebrities and it was not unusual to see a personality from film or television being shown around the buildings. Their involvement could be for a one-off fundraising venture or it could be more long term, as a regular supporter or a Vice President. Sometimes the meetings would be brief but sometimes there was time for a chat.

May 2008: Phil Tufnell: Phil was an England cricketer and one of the Vice Presidents of the Trust. He visited when Alby had only been at Tadworth Court for two weeks. Jimmy was also an avid sports fan and was delighted to meet one of his heroes.

December 2008: Danny Murphy: A coach from Fulham Football Club would regularly visit the Trust to give the children training sessions in wheelchair football. Danny made a special Christmas visit to the Trust and Alby was delighted to meet one of his footballing heroes.

February 2009: Gino de Campo: Chef Gino was running in the London Marathon to raise money for the Children's Trust and he went along to meet some of the children. Jim and Lisa met him in the Orange Room at the Cheyne Centre, although Lisa laughed later at the recollection that at the time she had never heard of Gino!

Cricket tournament: Mark Butcher: Mark, another England cricketer, was opening the outdoor practice nets at a local school and some of the children from The Children's Trust were invited along.

July 2009: Richard Hammond: Following his own recovery from an horrific head injury sustained during a high-speed car crash, television's Top Gear presenter and personality Richard was interested in the work of the Trust and opened two new buildings, Maple and Oak. Lisa and Alby met him in one of the corridors and cars quickly became the topic of conversation. Alby's physiotherapist Belinda took them to see the 43 year old Opel Kadett that Richard (the Hamster) Hammond had just bought in Botswana and had named Oliver.

Alby with Gino di Campo

Alby with Fulham players Danny Murphy, Julian Gray and Dickson Etuhu

Chapter 6
The Daily Mail

December 2008

"They want to write an article on Alby!" Lisa put the phone down and turned to Mark. "That was a journalist on the phone Mark. Marianne Power. She works for the Daily Mail. They've got hold of Alb's story and they want to do an article on him. The accident, his recovery, everything."

The journalist who interviewed Lisa and Mark was very understanding. She knew how much Alby and his family had been through and assured Lisa that the story would be handled sensitively. This would be a story in which the public would be interested. They would want to read about Alby's fight for life, his miraculous recovery.

Lisa and Mark told their story. The journalist asked questions and they answered. Lisa thought that it wouldn't be difficult to write about Alby and the way in which he was determined to pick up the threads of his life and weave them into the fabric of his future. Alby was becoming used to the limelight and couldn't wait to see what had been written about him.

Lisa grabbed the newspaper and her face fell as she read the headline. "Oh no! Mark," she wailed. "Look what they've written! The boy who wouldn't die! It's horrendous. I hate it. It sounds as if Alby's not done something he should have. What a nasty, horrible thing to put on the front page of a newspaper." Mark tried to reassure her.

"I think they were just trying to say that he'd defied the odds. I wouldn't worry about it. It's the story that's important, not the headline." When Lisa had calmed down she read the article and realised that Mark was right. The story had been reported accurately and showed Alby's courage and determination. Lisa realised that she couldn't really have asked for more. She still hated the headline.

Alby became even more of a local celebrity than he had been before. He seemed to take the newly acquired fame in his stride but inside he was excited and lapped up the attention. The newspaper carried several pictures of him – with Lisa, with Jimmy, before the accident and after the accident. He looked at the pictures. He couldn't remember the accident. People didn't think he could remember what happened before but he could and he looked at the pictures of himself and Jimmy. He smiled. *That was then*, he thought. *This is now*.

Chapter 7
Marathon Man

To Lisa's delight and amazement, Mark's determination to run the London Marathon on behalf of The Children's Trust didn't waiver once. He developed a rigorous training schedule to which he adhered, come rain or shine. Sometimes he didn't feel like going out and it would have been very easy to quit. He remembered Lisa's words – "You've never run for more than a bus" – and he realised the enormity of the challenge he had set himself. He'd always completely understood why mountaineers set themselves the challenge of a seemingly impossible climb, or trekkers tackle arctic conditions that few would embrace, let alone survive. He knew he shouldn't compare himself to people like that because usually they had years of experience and had worked towards their Big Challenge. He, on the other hand, had an ambition to go from zero running to the London Marathon without any interim personal challenges, without the stepping-stones of local runs or half marathons. But he did it without fear and without hesitation. "Madness," he told himself "but to hell with it. Why not?"

He researched the challenge that lay ahead of him and learned valuable tips.

Since he'd made the decision to run he'd had a year to get himself match-fit and in as good a shape as he could be. He hadn't realised then just how much work he would have to put in. He knew he couldn't just announce his desire to run and work up to it with a few circuits round the streets where he lived. To achieve a distance of 26.2miles required a dedicated programme of training, which included warm-ups before the start and stretching out at the end. He set about building up his distances and reducing his times. This helped to increase his endurance. It also required that he closely examine his eating habits, which he found needed a few tweaks to make it part of his programme. He had to put the right fuel into his body and the right balance of carbohydrate and protein was essential. He'd never been one to drink copious amounts of water but that became important too.

A typical day's training began at any time between 4.00am and 5.30am. Porridge became a staple on training days as it is a slow-release carbohydrate and would keep his energy levels stable for longer than would a sugary cereal. Mark finished his breakfast with a couple of slices of wholemeal toast. After his warm-up routine of stretches, a fast walk prepared his body and, to some extent, his mind for the serious business of running.

The family's attitude changed as they saw Mark's unswerving determination and their enthusiasm and admiration for him spurred him to greater heights, greater distances and shorter times. Their teasing had given way to encouragement and support.

The day of the run dawned. The weather was dry and the sky was clear. Mark knew that most runners prefer conditions to be cloudy but dry. The sun beating down on runners' heads may provide spectators with a perfect day but it could cause problems for those facing the challenge of a 26.2 mile run.

Mark's 2009 fundraising page told his story.

My stepson Alby is currently receiving rehab at The Children's Trust in Tadworth following a serious brain injury received after a road traffic accident. Since going there, his improvement has been nothing short of miraculous thanks to the amazing team of people working at the Trust.

Every penny raised will be put to good use.

Alby and Mark at a fundraiser for the London Marathon

Chapter 8
The London Marathon

Friday, 24 April 2009

"155,000 people! Can you imagine that? 155,000 people applied to run the Marathon this year." Mark looked up from the article he'd been reading.

Lisa looked back at him and gave a wry smile. "I take it they aren't all successful. How many places are actually given to people then?" Mark returned to the paper and scanned the rest of the article. "Apparently it's about 50,000. That's a hell of a lot of people, all in one place. Mind you, they won't always be in one place for long. I don't know how quickly I'll be able to shake off the competition but once I get into my stride the crowd should thin out a bit. I don't want to be tripping over anyone when I'm overtaking them, do I?"

Lisa shook her head, laughing as she handed Mark the tea towel. "Before you win and start charging for your autograph, perhaps you could dry these dishes. I see it as my job to stop fame going to your head. I think I need to keep you grounded – you know, keeping sight of your humble beginnings and all that. I'm just popping round to Mum's. She picked up some shopping for me at Lakeside yesterday and I said I'd nip over and collect it this morning." She planted a kiss on Mark's cheek and was gone.

As he dried the dishes, Mark pondered over the week ahead. Just two days until the race and he still had to train every day. Race? He mused over the word and decided it was really only a race for those who achieved the top places. For him and, he suspected, for a great many other participants, the achievement was probably in taking part in the first place and then just finishing.

Saturday, 25 April 2009

The early morning sun's rays played about Mark's head like puppies chasing a ball. Mark moved very slightly and then sat bolt upright. His first thought was "The Marathon! What have I done?" and he then sank back into his pillows as he realised it was not Sunday, it was only Saturday. Marathon fever had gripped the whole family and several of them had offered to go with Mark to the Excel Centre in London, just to collect his participant's pack which would include the number that he would later wear with pride. He mused on being fortunate in living close enough to London to be able to collect his pack and then return home. As he was to discover later, many entrants lived a significant distance from London and had to stay in or around the capital until the race the next day.

As Mark approached the Centre in London's Dockland he saw runners of all shapes and sizes at various stages of performance – some were stretching (it was hard to say whether they were setting out or returning), some were dousing themselves in water (obviously they'd returned) and some were sitting nervously on a wall, watching everyone else and doing a very good impression of not having any idea of what to do. Fellow runners smiled at him, many surrounded by their excited friends and family members, all chattering away about the minutia of the event. What time should we get to the finishing line? Will we be able to see you? Where should we stand? What shall we wave so you can see us?

Mark went to his collection point – as a novice entrant he had been allocated the pen for the slow runners. When Mark had been given a place the previous October, he'd had to give an estimate of the time he thought he would take. However, he'd been in training since then and six months had given him the chance to significantly improve on his original estimate but it wasn't possible to change. People round him were discussing the 'pens' system ('pen' as in cattle, not as in writing) and many wanted to change. Some had suffered injuries or hadn't been able to put in the training and wanted to transfer to a slower pen, some wanted to race with another person who had been allocated a different pen and some thought they'd improved on their time since completing the form so they wanted a change too. None of the appeals was successful. Mark thought it a little unfair.

The ballot for the race opened the day after the previous year's race and Mark didn't think he would get a place on his own, but because he was running for The Children's Trust they'd given him one of their places. People who run for a charity are much more likely to be given one of their allocated places but ask their runners to raise a minimum sum of money in return for their place. Mark had no trouble finding sponsors and asking them to donate via the internet through Justgiving made the whole process a lot easier than asking people to sign up and then having to collect their money after the event. Mark found out that for the London Marathon, Justgiving made no commission deduction, which was good to know. About 750 charities have guaranteed places every year and another 550 are given a place every five years. Mark mused on the opportunity that offered for raising a great deal of money for good causes and felt proud to be a part of such a worthwhile event.

Home for one last training session before tomorrow. Mark Walsh. From couch potato to 26.2 miles. That's an achievement, thought Mark. He reigned himself in. *You haven't done it yet and you...* but he wouldn't let himself finish the thought that he might not complete the course. Adrenalin raced through his body every time he thought of the enormity of the task ahead of him. He'd need that adrenalin tomorrow and it was a pity he couldn't bottle it now and use it tomorrow. As they journeyed home Lisa outlined all her plans to help him.

"A good dinner tonight, then lots of slow release carbs tomorrow. That's right, isn't it?" Mark nodded. He needed all the help he could get.

Sunday, 26 April 2009

A misty daybreak soon gave way to brilliant sunshine and the optimistic encouragement that members of the family were giving Mark was vying for dominance over the tension in the Walsh/Dobinson household. It was decided that Mark would travel alone to the start line, with Lisa and the rest of the family travelling later to encourage him from the sidelines. Breakfast of porridge, bananas and wholemeal toast finished, Mark made his way to Greenwich at 7.30am for the start of the race. Although the start line was in Blackheath, due to the staggered starts Mark had been advised to go to Greenwich or Maze Hill station. There wasn't a specific "On your marks, get set, go!" There were too many runners for that to be a viable or safe option. They left in swathes, according to their allocated pen. Individual times were recorded via a chip worn by each runner and that chip wouldn't be activated until the runner passed the start line. Mark found the red pen and his section.

"First time mate?" asked a red-haired man with an exceptionally broad grin. Mark nodded. "This is my eighth London Marathon," came the reply, "and my twelfth marathon overall. I've done Berlin, Dublin, Paris and Edinburgh too. It's a great feeling. You'll love it!" Mark must have looked perplexed. "Oh, you're wondering why I'm in this pen, then. Ah well, long story short I buggered my knee during the last Paris run and it's really affected my time. I didn't want to pull out so I just thought I'd sort of take it easy this time. Might even prevent me from hitting that wall again."

"I'm sorry," Mark ventured, "hitting what wall? Sounds painful. Is that what caused the knee injury? Didn't you see it or something?" The man looked at Mark, with an avuncular smile.

"No, not an actual wall. It's what we say when we get to that point when we just can't carry on anymore. Or we think we can't. But we do. I've run marathons and never hit a wall, then sometimes it can come quite early on. Last time it was at the 17 mile mark."

"Oh my goodness. What do you do? Do you have to stop, or call it a day, or what?"

"You slow a bit and then you start thinking of all the reasons why you're doing it and whether you're aiming for a PB. That can make a difference. It seems like it's in your bloody legs, but it's really in your mind."

"PB?" Mark was really beginning to feel as though he hadn't a clue what he'd let himself in for.

"PB is Personal Best. You never really know when you're going to achieve it. So much depends on other factors that you can't anticipate. Hitting that bloody wall is one, then there's what physical shape you're in. I ran once with a pretty heavy cold and the whole thing was rubbish from start to finish. But I did finish and that was what was important on the day. I forgot about a PB 'cos I think it was my Personal Worst. You just can't tell."

Mark watched as the man stretched out and did some peculiar little jumps. Stretching before running was important to loosen up the muscles and stretching afterward was to drain any lactic acid build-up in calves, thighs and hamstrings. Without that, there is a risk of severe cramps and muscle pain that could take hours or sometimes days to disappear. Mark had picked up loads of useful tips from the Runners' World magazine. He had originally bought the magazine out of curiosity and it had opened up a whole new world for him. The magazine contained training programmes for beginners, intermediate and advanced runners. Even the one for beginners looked daunting but Mark thought about the Chinese saying, "A journey of a thousand miles begins with one step." In fact, Mark had been told that the saying should be correctly translated as, "A journey of a thousand miles begins under one's feet." He thought it very appropriate. He'd not given a thought to the fact that the running wouldn't just exercise his body but also his heart and people could go from a 65-70 heart resting rate to a 46-48 after some serious training. He felt that his lung capacity had increased significantly and he was managing some very long distances without feeling any strain.

He had begun his serious training regime four months previously (as recommended by Runners' World), rising very early to run before he had to leave for work. He never knew what time he'd get home at night and the winter months weren't the most welcoming in the late afternoon and early evening. Despite high visibility clothing, Mark detested running at night. He'd had to do it occasionally and was always amazed that although he had had to force himself to go out after work, often feeling very tired, within a few minutes he felt energised and refreshed. His average training session covered ten miles and he gradually increased this as April approached.

It was only 8.00am and his pen wasn't setting off until 10.30am. Mark checked his watch several times. A middle-aged woman looked at him. "You look like a rabbit caught in head-lights. It must be your first marathon. Me too. Awful, isn't it?" She laughed. Mark nodded. He could see she was running for Cancer Research. She must have read his thoughts because before he could say anything she noticed Mark looking at her T-shirt. "I lost my husband two years ago. We used to run together and I thought what better way of honouring his memory than doing this. He was always ten times better than me and I never thought that I'd..." She looked at the floor and then back at Mark. "I don't recognise your shirt. Sorry." Mark told her about Alby and explained why he wanted to help The Children's Trust. He also confessed to feeling nervous so she was in good company. "I expect you'll be faster than me – you've got longer legs. I'm only five foot one and I seem to have to do more steps to cover the same distance as someone as tall as you!" She giggled and offered Mark her hand. "Pat," she said.

"Mark, pleased to meet you, five foot one Pat! We can encourage each other."

"Oh, you'll be over the horizon long before me," she mused, "but good luck anyway. I'll just be happy to finish." Mark had read stories in the magazine about runners who'd forged friendships during the race and he was beginning to understand that now. You could almost taste the tension it was so thick and the emotion in the atmosphere seemed to match it in bucketloads. He could hear other runners exchanging stories about why they were running. They were all touching and deeply personal. He was glad Lisa couldn't hear them – she'd be crying all day.

"Jeez! 26 miles! I need my bloody bumps felt!" boomed a deep voice a few feet away from Mark. "Aw, shut-up Rory. Never mind the Marathon, you need your bloody bumps felt anyway. Here, gi' us a feel then!" Mark looked up to catch a glimpse of two men and, judging by the accent, they were Scotsmen. They were both bearded, both dressed in tartan kilts and one was sporting a tartan bra, complete with filling and tassels. The 'man' was grabbing the 'female's' bra. "Och! Keep your dirty feelers off ma tits mon!" The other runners who heard this exchange laughed. The men were two of very many who were running in fancy dress. It wasn't obvious from their garb just who they were running for but seeing all eyes on them the 'female' said that they were brothers and they'd lost their mum to Motor Neurone Disease. Their laughter disappeared instantly, as if they'd sobered up after a night out. "I don't think anyone should go through what our Ma suffered. We wanted to help stop that. It's a filthy, unnecessary waste of life. The indignity is the worst bit." They didn't go any further, but Mark knew what they meant. He'd met someone who had nursed people with MND and knew just how dreadful it was, especially towards the end of life.

Mark suddenly realised that as the sun was rising in the sky so was the temperature. He had a cap in case it became unbearably hot but Spring sunshine was always welcome. A number of other runners were commenting on the increasing heat. "No one wants it to rain or, worse still, rain *and* wind but the heat can make things hard." Mark turned and nodded to the woman who had spoken to him. "It's not so bad at first," she continued seemingly oblivious to whether or not she had captured Mark's attention, "but when you get some of the bottle necks it's hard not to lose your rag when it's really hot. Around the docks some of the streets are so bloody narrow we just can't all get through and you have to walk. The sun hits the buildings and reflects down to the street so it's bloody hot! It makes you so glad to get through it and start up your own pace again." Mark thanked her for the advice, wondering why she was in the same pen as him if she was an experienced runner. Before he could ask she smiled and said, "I sort of hope it is like that so I can slow down a bit, you know, a kind of enforced rest. I hope the guy was right." Mark obviously looked puzzled. "Oh, I don't know about it myself. This is my first time. I spoke to this guy Darren yesterday at Excel. It's all really new to me but he's done it before, loads of times and I guess it's good to share your experiences. I don't think he was trying to put me off, just sort of let me know it's not plain sailing."

"Have you travelled far?" asked Mark.

"Maidstone, in Kent. I stayed at the Premier Inn last night. You?"

"Oh no, I'm near enough to travel in today. Less time to worry about it. Harold Wood, in Essex."

"Darren came from Sudbury. I think he said it was in Suffolk. Another woman in the queue had come down from Manchester. Darren said that some people even come from abroad. That level of enthusiasm has to be admired!"

"Well, they'll all deffo be a hundred times better than me," confessed Mark. Before they could continue their conversation they were called to their starting point. Mark felt as ready as he'd ever be and totally unprepared, all at the same time. He hardly knew what had happened but suddenly he was running. Most people had been in the same red pen as Mark. He didn't even see the runners in the blue pen (people who run for clubs and those who had been successful in gaining a place in the ballot) or the green pen (people whose times were good for their age – known as GFAs, those with exceptional running times, and famous people). The red pen was for everyone else, including those like Mark who had been given charity places. Even then, they were split into eight different sections. The enormity of it all was quite overwhelming.

His pace was steady. "Not a sprint, a marathon," he told himself. There were people all around him. Close. Very close. He was hemmed in but he could have been completely alone as his thoughts meandered through his mind. He thought about why he was doing this. He thought about Alby and his determination to dismiss the very crappy hand that life had dealt his stepson. Mark himself had received much admiration (and fortunately a great deal of sponsorship) for his determination to run this course but he felt that it was absolutely nothing compared with Alby's courage and strength of character. His mind then ceased its wandering and settled in Alby's room at Tadworth Court. Mark watched the stream of professionals as they passed through the room. The consultants, doctors, nurses, physiotherapy and occupational health teams, office staff, porters and cleaners – in fact, everyone who had played even the smallest part in Alby's recovery.

Before he had a chance for further reflection, he realised he had reached the docks area and he was in the shadow of the huge office blocks and people were crowding in on one another. Canary Wharf, the Cutty Sark and the road narrowed. *So this is the bottle neck*, thought Mark. Fortunately, there was a stopping point nearby and some runners were taking the opportunity that the enforced slower pace had afforded them and were taking onboard some much-needed fluid.

Mark then noticed that the crowds were cheering and calling out the names of individual runners. The runners directed smiles and waves towards the crowd, everyone caught up in the atmosphere of the event. Mark was sure that runners would find it very difficult to spot their own supporters whilst they were running unless, of course, the supporters had managed to grab a place right at the edge of the course, or against some of the barriers that separated them from the runners. The crowd was also very dense in places, and Mark guessed that everyone was just grateful for the level of support they were being given – runners and crowd alike. After all, supporters knew that the runners had all set themselves a very tough physical challenge and were probably showing their appreciation for the months of slog through training, the money raised and the eventual good that would come of all this combined effort. His musing stopped when he spotted Lisa, leaning over Alby's wheelchair to make a huge noise banging the barriers with brightly coloured sticks. It seemed everybody was doing the same. They shouted, cheered and waved, screaming his name as he passed them. All Mark could do was to smile at them and wave. He daren't stop.

Regaining his pace fifteen minutes later Mark realised that his nervousness had actually been replaced by nervous energy. He thought that adrenalin came in short bursts but he guessed that the immense stress under which he'd placed himself both emotionally and physically had just enabled that adrenalin to keep pumping through him. He certainly felt its effect.

Mark didn't feel at all tired as he approached the halfway point and wondered if he'd experience a negative split. He thought that would be fantastic for his first marathon, although he suddenly realised that he'd not really given any thought to any others in the future. He'd overheard a conversation at Excel yesterday and knew that a negative split was the term for running the second half faster than the first. Perhaps that was a good thing. Holding yourself back in the first half would certainly keep energy reserves for the final push but, as far as he was concerned, Mark thought it was highly unlikely. He knew tiredness would catch up with him eventually and as soon as the thought came to him he realised that it had probably just set in.

The man running next to him starting talking in short gasps, keeping rhythm with his running pace. "We're over halfway now," he said, "Got to keep going. Can't stop now!" Mark wasn't sure if the man was actually talking to him or whether he was trying to convince himself but it didn't matter. The man's words echoed around Mark's head as a truth he could not ignore. "Can't stop now. So much at stake. Don't want to let Alby down. Don't want to let Lisa down. Don't want to let myself down." With those thoughts bouncing around him, Mark ploughed on with renewed spirit if not with renewed strength. His legs were beginning to feel this run like they'd never felt during any run before, even the longest one that he had called his dress rehearsal but even that wasn't the full 26.2 miles. He'd read advice on the London Marathon website which said that for most runners the second half was the real marathon challenge and he was beginning to understand why. If you'd trained properly the first half wasn't too difficult but the second half was a completely different ball game.

Mark's family left Canary Wharf and headed for Westminster, determined to give Mark as much support as they could. They hadn't realised that there was no wheelchair access at Westminster, so Jim carried Alby up the escalator and Jimmy carried the wheelchair. They couldn't stop themselves laughing at the chaos they were causing but nobody seemed to care. They were glad it was a Sunday and there were no commuters to get annoyed with them.

As he approached Westminster, knowing that the end was in sight, Mark saw the gang again and he wasn't sure if they could make any more noise! Clapping, cheering, shouting, screaming and banging the barriers – all for him. He felt overwhelmed by their support and their huge love. He felt a great surge of gratitude for all the positivity in his life, despite the lousy hand that had been dealt to Alby.

He just needed to finish. He knew he was slowing but he wouldn't stop. If he rested, even for minute his legs would seize up. The wind was picking up now and if it got behind you it helped but running into the wind was not something Mark wanted to encounter at such a late stage. Fortunately, it was mostly behind him. Suddenly, Pall Mall came into view. Mark found it the longest, hardest but most rewarding stretch. He was conscious of tears welling up behind his eyes. Would they free themselves and join the sweat on his face? Mark didn't care. He was finishing........and suddenly he'd done it! He was over the finish line. 6 hours, 4 minutes, 47 seconds.

His legs were aching and shaking, his head hurt, he was emotionally overwhelmed and he just wanted to sit down. He was guided by officials who were praising his effort but at the same time showing him where to go. He'd arranged to meet Lisa in St James Park but looking at the size of it he wondered if they would find each other. He pulled out his phone and rang Lisa. It was over.

Mark had done it. He had completed the London Marathon. He had raised £2,570.00.

Spurred on by his success in the Marathon, on 31 May 2010 he ran the London Bupa 10K. Mark laughed as he thought about it. "Compared with the London Marathon, it was a walk in the park!"

Alby with Lisa, Jimmy and Mark at the London Marathon

Chapter 9
Home

January 2009

Alby was walking with the aid of a frame. He was wobbly and unsure, but he was walking. Indoors he didn't need his wheelchair as he could get wherever he need to be, albeit very slowly.

April 2009

When Alby came home, whether it was in six weeks or six months, he was going to need help. Lisa and Mark realised that their home would have to be adapted to accommodate Alby. Plans were drawn up and eventually work began creating an extension right across the back of the house. Half of it would be a bedroom for Alby, which would lead into an ensuite bathroom, complete with hoist for lowering Alby into the bath. This would be created from what had been the kitchen. The other half of the extension would form a new kitchen. They were fortunate that there was room to build the extension. They didn't want to move house, adding further disruption to their lives and Alby had had disruption enough for a lifetime.

Time was of the essence with this project and, with the help of understanding builders, the alterations were complete before Alby finally returned home.

Chapter 10
Return to School

Spring 2009

A new phenomenon had appeared. Its first manifestation was at Tadworth and then it appeared at Alby's home. This phenomenon was the Alby Effect – the extraordinary way in which people found themselves affected by an extraordinary young man. At Tadworth Court hospital staff who'd only had the briefest of contact with Alby shed tears of joy when he spoke for the first time. At home, neighbours had awaited Alby's return with anticipation that bordered on sheer excitement. There was a genuine outpouring of love and admiration for the magnificent fighting machine that Alby had become. Shenfield High School became the latest place to experience the Alby Effect when Alby returned to school in the Spring of 2009.

Lisa had been asked if she wanted Alby to attend a special school – a school that would cater for his disabilities, a school that would be used to dealing with wheelchairs, physical impairment and special educational needs. Lisa refused. She wanted Alby to return to his old school – a school he knew, a school that knew him, a school that knew all about him. Shenfield had a Special Educational Needs department and Lisa had every faith that they could and would support Alby and respond to all his needs. The headteacher, John, also had faith that his Special Educational Needs department and its Co-ordinator, Jan, could and would provide the best possible environment for Alby and for his return to full-time education.

Shenfield High School came under Essex Education Authority's jurisdiction but Alby lived within the area covered by the London Borough of Havering. So, preliminary meetings were arranged between Anna, Head of Special Needs at Havering's Education Department and staff at the school – Jane, Pastoral Manager at Shenfield High School, and Jan. Lisa, Mark and Alby also met with all the educational professionals who were involved in Alby's rehabilitation. Alby chose his own curriculum with the help of Jane and Linda, his Head of Year. It was a full curriculum of all the core subjects – English, Maths, Science, Health and Social Care, IT and Business Studies. Only time would tell if Alby would be able to manage it but, for the time being, he was testing the waters of school by going in for one day a week. The plan was that Alby would begin by attending school just one day a week in order to adjust to as much of the daily routine as he could manage. If things went well, he would then return full time in September, re-joining his own year group. There were no plans to hold him back nor any suggestion that he join a lower year group. Monthly meetings were held to gauge his progress. For some time, disability discrimination legislation had slowly been making organisations aware of the situation of those using a wheelchair and Shenfield High School presented no problems for Alby. Thanks to the lifts and ramps, no area of the school was inaccessible to him.

April 2009

Shenfield High School: Jane

Jane, as Alby's Pastoral Manager, could not have been more helpful or determined that everything that Alby needed would be provided. So, once a week, Alby went back to his old school.

Jane and Jan (the Special Educational Needs Co-ordinator) worked closely with Lisa, The Children's Trust and Havering and Essex Education authorities to prepare a package of care and a curriculum for Alby. Lisa and Mark attended monthly meetings to evaluate progress and everything seemed to be running smoothly. The only disagreement that they had during those difficult months was when Lisa objected to the suggestion that Alby's personal care (toileting and the like) could be dealt with by anyone who was available. She would preserve her son's dignity at any cost and making his personal care another task that could be dealt with by anyone was certainly not what she had in mind – and she didn't hesitate to voice her concerns.

Sarah and Anita were appointed as teaching assistants and, as they were friends outside school, it was felt that they would work highly effectively as a team within school. They were employed specifically for Alby and their sole responsibility was his care. He needed assistance with everything – moving from one chair to another, using the toilet, eating, drinking, reading and writing.

The school already had a student who needed help with toileting. He could manage himself if he was handed what he needed but required assistance getting to and from the toilet. Alby's needs were completely different and he was totally dependent on his carers for his all his needs. Personal care formed part of Anita and Sarah's contracts. As the school grew in confidence over dealing with students with complex needs, the number of students with those needs grew. As a result of this, personal care eventually formed part of the contract of every Learning Support Assistant (LSA).

Although Alby's ability to read had not been completely lost, such was the extent of his brain injury he could not understand much of what he was reading and Anita modified texts for him by simplifying words. For example, changing 'dejected' to 'sad'. Alby also had little speech and staff learned to interpret the sounds he made. Alby soon trained the staff in his ways, using a mixture of pointing and guttural sounds, slowly forming words to let those around him know what he wanted.

Friends who had known Alby before the accident would spend their break and lunchtimes with him, chatting and laughing. The Alby Effect slowly enveloped staff and pupils. Like an all pervasive mist it crept everywhere. It wasn't long before every improvement, every act of determination and every change, no matter how small, was given public recognition – always verbally and sometimes with cheering and clapping! Alby basked in the approval of his teachers and peers. He didn't just grin. His face was transformed by a smile so wide and so powerful it was impossible not to feel its blinding effect. Gradually, some of the sounds Alby made were changing into words and he found it easier to communicate with those around him.

Alby was glad to see all his old school friends again. The one day a week he spent at school left him exhausted but happy. It was very tiring and it taxed him physically and mentally to the extent that when he returned home at the end of a school day all he wanted to do was sleep – after dinner of course.

September 2009

September is always a time for change in the Halls of Academia. Owing to contractual restrictions, teaching staff can only change schools at certain times in the academic year, the most popular time being September. Just before Alby's full-time return to Shenfield High School, there were staff changes and Jan, the Special Educational Needs Co-ordinator, retired.

Tony

An English teacher by trade, Tony became the school's Special Educational Needs Co-ordinator (known in educational circles as the SENCO). Tony had been offered the position of SENCO a few months earlier. At that time, schools often had difficulty filling the role of SENCO and it wasn't uncommon for a teacher of just about any subject to take on the additional responsibility of SENCO. Tony approached his new role with apparently limitless reserves of energy and enthusiasm. However, Alby's reintegration into school scared the living daylights out of Tony who felt that he didn't have the knowledge or experience to pull it off. He knew of Alby but had never met him. The responsibility of the task that lay ahead of him weighed him down. He was terrified that somehow or in some way, Alby would be disadvantaged by that inexperience and that the provision offered by Shenfield High School would be hopelessly inadequate. "I didn't have the knowledge and the skills to be able to say definitely 'this is what we do and this is how we do it.' There were going to be bumps along the way and I think we all knew that. We had to rip up the rule book and start again. We had to look at individual scenarios."

Tony knew that the Education Authority had told Lisa that Alby should attend a special school, where premises and curriculum had already been adapted for other children. That was not going to happen on Lisa's watch and Tony knew that he was dealing with one feisty lady who was not going to back down or roll over for anyone, least of all a rookie SENCO. Headteacher John was more than happy for Alby to return full time and told Tony, "He's coming back full time – sort it! What do you need?"

Tony needed to get his own handle on the arrangements which had been put into place for Alby so the round of phone calls between Tony and The Children's Trust, Havering Education Authority and a number of Essex healthcare professionals began. Specialist teachers all made suggestions and gradually Tony began to feel that the blanket of expertise and knowledge that he lacked was beginning to surround him – and it felt good. Perhaps it was the grown up version of a child's security blanket and it was certainly working.

Tony had to look at what was needed and what could be offered. Could Alby do GCSEs? Would he need a bespoke curriculum for that? What should he do? The thought of letting Alby down crossed Tony's mind and was dismissed as quickly as it had formed. That definitely wasn't an option and so began the first of many conversations with Lisa and Mark – initially with Lisa.

Alby had to learn to write and speak. Tony was faced with a myriad of questions, some of which he knew were completely unanswerable. Could Alby take any General Certificate of Secondary Education (GCSE) examinations? If so, in which subjects? He would almost certainly need help. He would need special exam access arrangements – help with writing, reading, extra time, supervised rest breaks, prompts and oral language modification. Tony worked tirelessly to ensure that Alby had as much help as was available. Some of it came through Havering and some through Essex. Tony had never had any dealings with Havering but it soon became clear that they didn't work in the same way as Essex. They had different criteria and different priorities. Tony was familiar and more comfortable with Essex Education Authority's way of working. Specialist teachers would come into school to deal with specific needs – neurological impairment, vocal problems, hearing or extreme physical problems. Sometimes they would advise staff on the way in which a student's needs should be met and sometimes a specialist teacher would come into school to deal directly with the student.

Another Shenfield student, Rebecca, had also received rehabilitation at The Children's Trust and she and Alby returned to school at the same time. Her needs were not as complex as Alby's but it was good for Alby to feel that he was not on his own. A specialist teacher from Essex, Hannah, came to school to teach her. Tony felt very frustrated by a system that precluded Hannah from helping Alby because he came under a different authority. Sometimes, when everyone was seated round a table discussing the other student's needs, Tony was able to glean advice which could be easily transferred to Alby without directly going against any protocols.

Havering was a much larger authority than Essex and funding was never an issue. The Physical and Neurological Impairment Team advised on all aspects of Alby's needs, including whether or not a specialist teacher would be needed but it was felt that with support from his LSAs and teaching staff, Alby could manage without.

Alby gave every ounce of energy he could muster to his schoolwork. He could not yet write and he would communicate through his teaching assistants who would scribe for him. He had a few free periods each week and used the time to complete his homework – as far as possible, Alby wanted to be the same as the other students. It was very tiring and if Alby ran out of steam, Lisa would come to the school and take him home. It was a situation that Alby would later use to his own advantage.

October 2009

Glynn

Tony needed an assistant Special Educational Needs Co-ordinator and the school's advertisement was answered by a man who had met Tony on a course some years previously. Glynn fulfilled all their criteria and had much more experience in the area of special needs than any other candidate, so was appointed Assistant Co-ordinator of the Pupil and Administration Support Service. As soon as he met Alby they formed a strong bond and later, when Alby had relearned the skill to write, his first successful attempt was in the form of a note to Glynn. Large, childlike letters spelled out the words: "Do you know who this is? Do you?"

The significance of that milestone was not lost on Glynn who told Alby, "I promise you I'll always keep this note." He kept that promise.

Alby's Learning Support Assistant, Anita, left the school the following term in order to train as a social worker and her friend and colleague Sarah soon followed. Their places were taken by Anna, a former care home assistant, and Jacqui, a qualified nurse. A good working relationship with Alby was soon established but as Alby gained in strength and confidence so he began to push the boundaries. Fortunately, Anna and Jacqui ruled with rods of iron wrapped in velvet and took no nonsense from their charge. There was a determination that, as far as possible, Alby would be treated like any other student. It would have been very easy to indulge him and to make not only special arrangements but also to make allowances for him in ways that would not benefit him. It soon became clear that he intended to act just like any other student and push his teachers as far as he could.

Alby

Alby was absolutely delighted with his new wheelchair. It was like nothing he had used before. *"How could you compare a bicycle with a Harley Davison motor bike?"* thought Alby as he switched through the chair's five speeds. He might not be able to walk but he was certainly not going to be held back and at every opportunity he switched to the highest speed. Unfortunately, his teachers thought otherwise and gave Alby the strictest instruction to use only the first three speeds. Compliance with this was spasmodic within the school buildings but being outside gave Alby many opportunities to defy the rules. On one occasion he was observed operating his wheelchair at the highest speed and at the same time giving two of his friends rides on the back. He was apprehended by a teacher who only just managed to get out of the way before he was mown down.

One day, Alby and his friend Tyler decided to play trains with their wheelchairs. Alby was the driver in his motorised 'chair and Tyler in his manual 'chair became the carriage in this fantasy train. Tyler held onto the back of Alby's 'chair and Alby set off, blasting his horn at anyone who had the temerity to get in their way. The two of them charged across the playground, using the banned fifth speed. Students laughed and cheered as the train ploughed through the lunchtime groups. Lunchtime assistants ran after them but no one was able to catch them. When challenged about it later, two innocent faces looked shocked that anyone could think them capable of such behaviour.

Not long after that Alby defied a school ban on the use of the school playing field – a sanction usually imposed because of wet weather having turned it into a bog. Alby discovered that it wasn't so boggy when it was frozen, which made a little jaunt over its wide open space, free of other people, very inviting. Alby had just got into his stride and was enjoying the freedom and the feel of the wind in his face when he was spotted by a teacher. *They're always trying to spoil my fun,* thought Alby and conveniently pretended that he didn't hear the instruction to leave the field. He knew he'd be for it but figured it would be worth it. He was put on report, which meant that teachers had to report on his behaviour every lesson. *Being on report is for naughty boys*, thought Alby, *and I'm one!* Lisa was not amused.

It was 28 September and Alby asked to stay at home instead of going to school. It was Lisa's birthday and not only that, Jim and Linda were moving house. Alby didn't want to miss anything and if he went to school he would miss a great deal but Lisa insisted that he should go to school. "You've missed enough schooling already Alby and everyone will be here when you come home from school." Later that morning Lisa received a phone call from the school.

"Alby is not well," said the school's medical officer. "He has stomach pains and is in a great deal of discomfort. He is clearly unwell. He's also extremely tired. We feel that he should come home." Lisa collected Alby. She strapped him into his seat and looked in the rear view mirror. Her clearly unwell son was grinning as he asked his mother how Jim and Linda's move was going.

As time progressed, Alby's needs were reviewed. After one of the regular review meetings between staff, an occupational therapist and physiotherapist, everyone congregated in the Special Needs teaching area for a coffee break. The meeting concerned Alby's use of his wheelchair and how much encouragement he would need to continue in his efforts to walk. Alby had listened them discussing his progress. They had based their comments on what they'd seen but he knew much more than they did. He knew how determined he was. Quietly, he opened his can of drink and ate his chocolate bar and crisps. He sipped his drink, listening intently. How much help would Alby need to move from his wheelchair to a table? How many times a day should Alby be expected to use his legs before he became too tired? Alby finished his drink and slowly began to push his chair away from the table. Unusually, silence descended. There was no reason for everyone to fall silent but they did. There was expectation hanging in the air. All eyes turned to Alby but no one knew why. Alby stood up and picked up his wrappers and empty can from the table. He turned away from the table and walked slowly to the bin – a distance of about five metres. He threw everything into the bin, turned and walked back to his seat. Tony sat open-mouthed. No one said a word. Then came the eruption. Clapping and shouts of, "Well done, Albs!" and, "Oh my goodness! What did you just do?" filled the room. Alby was walking.

Tony

Tony retreated to his office, sat down, put his head in his hands and cried for ten minutes. "It was one of the most magical things I've ever seen. It was like watching a child walk unaided for the first time. It was the same feeling of euphoria. The difference here was that with a child you expect walking to happen eventually, but with Alby you never knew when or even if it would happen." Unashamed of his reaction, Tony wiped his face and returned to the teaching area, where he was met with one of Alby's huge and rather special grins. "You've done it again, you! You've made me cry!"

Some lessons contained sensitive subjects. Tony made sure that if any lesson content was likely to upset Alby he would be forewarned and allowed to opt out of that lesson if he so chose. Personal, Social and Health Education (PSHE) or Citizenship lessons could deal with road safety issues and Health and Social Care lessons could deal with brain injury and its effects. Alby never opted out. He took everything in his stride. He had accepted his injuries and subsequent disabilities as though they were part of the pattern of life. He was rarely heard to complain or rail against the unfairness of his misfortune. Only once did Lisa hear him use expletives about the woman who had knocked him down. She had never seen Alby display such unreserved anger but it was very short-lived and Alby soon realised he had to move on. In fact, when Lisa found herself overcome with emotion about what had happened, Alby would put his hand on her arm and tell her, "Mum, I've accepted what happened and now you need to."

Tony's Year 7 tutor group was in a PSHE lesson with the rest of the year group and a theatre company was in school to make a presentation on road safety. Alby was in a higher year group and was not there. To accommodate the number of students, the lesson was in the hall. The group gave a very moving performance showing a young girl being knocked down by a car. The sound effects of screeching brakes were very realistic and Tony found it was too much. Overcome with emotion, he left the hall and went to his office. He took some time and a coffee to get over the effect of the performance and returned to the hall. The Head of Year approached him with a smile. "Don't worry," she said, "I understand."

"I wasn't there when Alby had his accident but it has affected me in ways I couldn't have imagined," said Tony. "The effect that he had on the school, the staff and the students, was profound. He used to come into my office and transform it. He would sit down on one of my chairs and we'd put some music on and just chill. It was unbelievable. When life throws me something nasty or unexpected, I always think of Albs and what he's been through. I think of how he's coped and I tell myself to shut up and get on with it! No other student has ever affected me like that and the Alby Effect will stay with me forever."

Exams

The aim was to help Alby achieve as much as possible and that included taking his GCSEs and a B-Tec in Health and Social Care. (The Business and Technology Education Council offer qualifications, called B-Tecs, in a variety of subjects.) Alby had a Statement of Educational Needs – a legal document that entitled him to all kinds of help. He had modified furniture, chairs, an iPad and a speech aid as well as simple aids like a walking frame. Glynn and Anna had been on a course to learn Makaton sign language and this proved to be an invaluable communication aid. Alby was allowed 100% extra time for his exams. He could have the text modified, he could have a scribe and he could have supervised rest breaks. He didn't always need them but they were there if he did. Alby successfully sat his GCSEs in English, Maths and Information Technology. He also gained his B-Tec in Health and Social Care.

Sports Day – 2010

A group of Alby's friends went to see Garry, the Head of Physical Education, because they wanted Alby to be able to take part in the forthcoming Sports Day. "We want something for Alby to do, otherwise it's not fair if he can't take part." Before the accident, Alby had been a keen sportsman and his friends knew that Alby's disability meant he would not be able to be a part of Sports Day – well, not in the way in which he used to take part.

"Yes, I'm up for that," replied Garry. "You come up with something for him and I'll look at it. Tell me what you want and I'll put it in the programme." Anoop, Tommy and Charlie put their heads together and devised a plan. Alby knew nothing about it until Sports Day arrived and his friends encouraged him to enter the 100 metre race. Alby, Anoop, Charlie, Tommy and some other students from their year stood at the starting line. Garry fired the starting gun and off they went. Most students kept behind Alby but occasionally one of his friends overtook him and then deliberately held back to allow Alby to be in front. Nearing the finishing line, Tommy surged forward and looked set to win when Charlie shouted, "You ain't doing that!" and rugby tackled Tommy to the floor. Alby walked through the finishing line to the loudest and longest roar that the school had ever heard. The clapping and cheering continued for several minutes and Alby was awarded the winner's medal. This time it was Alby who was overcome with emotion.

Alby's friends would often come into the Special Needs area at break and lunchtimes and as Alby's walking improved they took him outside the play football. Anna and Jacqui frequently accompanied them. In 2011 two new Learning Support Assistants joined the staff. Michael and James were both in their early twenties and, being very keen sportsmen, they didn't need any persuading to join Team Alby for football. The atmosphere in the school's SEN department that summer was the happiest that many of the teachers had ever experienced and it was all due to the Alby Effect.

Alby back at school playing football

Chapter 11
The Second Skin

August 2009

Alby was sent to Camden in north London to be measured for a spinal jacket help to keep his torso upright and his spine straight. The doctors were worried that Alby's all-round lack of strength would lead to curvature of the spine and put pressure on his internal organs.

Lisa trusted the staff to do what was necessary but the second skin reminded her of something from a torture chamber. It also reminded Lisa of a wetsuit worn by divers but it contained rigid strips, like a Victorian corset. It was so tight that it was a struggle to get it on Alby. It was in two pieces, which zipped together at the side. When it was on, it made him very hot – sometimes unbearably hot – and, although she hated it, with a smile that belied her true feelings Lisa encouraged him to persevere. Warm days were obviously the worst. Everyone was wearing T-shirts and shorts but Alby was encased in his own personal sauna. He had to wear it for 24 hours a day. The only respite came when it needed to be washed. It was cumbersome enough when dry, but when saturated with water it was heavy and almost impossible to lift. It couldn't be dried in a machine and took several hours to drip dry. Alby was to continue wearing his second skin until the Autumn of 2011.

Following his return home, all Alby's therapies were conducted at the Harold Hill Health Centre which was not far from his home in Harold Wood. In the Autumn of 2011 the physiotherapist at Harold Wood decided Alby was strong enough to cope without the help of his second skin. It had done its job and Alby's spine was straight. Lisa breathed a sigh of relief when she ritualistically disposed of it, praising and cursing it all at the same time. However, she was immensely pleased that it had worked.

Chapter 12
Olympic Fever, 2012

Glynn

When Glynn joined Shenfield High School as the Assistant Co-ordinator of the Pupil Administration and Support Service, Alby had been back in main stream schooling for six months. Glynn already had many years' experience of helping students with special needs and was aware of Alby's background. He was determined to leave no stone unturned in his quest to find as much support as possible for this gallant young fighter.

It was Monday morning and Glynn looked at his email inbox. There were in excess of 40 messages and most had been sent over the weekend. He wondered whether some of his colleagues actually thought about anything but work. Did they not have other things to do at weekends? Weekends should be sacrosanct. Perhaps they were trying to outdo each other in a bid to send the highest number of weekend emails. He sighed.

There was a higher than usual proportion of advertising emails and as Glynn flicked through them, giving most just a cursory glance, one caught his eye. Lloyds TSB had sent an email asking for nominations for torch bearers for the Paralympic Games – the Olympic Games for people with a disability and the title had morphed into 'Paralympic'. Just as he was about to delete the message, Glynn thought, *Alby could do that.* Carrying the torch was an honour, a privilege, prestigious.

Glynn looked at the online application form and stared out of the window. After a minute he turned back to his desk and began typing. "How on earth am I going to do this?" he asked himself. He'd seen a newspaper article about nominations to carry the Paralympic torch, so asked Lisa for permission to nominate Alby. Lisa was delighted to give her consent and was bubbling with excitement just at the thought that Glynn's application might be successful. Glynn had exactly 100 words in which to say why he felt that Alby deserved to carry the torch through part of its journey. Glynn did not consider himself proficient enough with words to pare down Alby's journey without detracting from the enormity of his achievements. Carefully wording his application, Glynn struggled with condensing everything into a short paragraph. "How do you get it all into such a small space? What do you leave out? Would leaving out any aspect of Alby's remarkable journey dilute its importance?" Eventually, after many rewrites, Glynn finally submitted the application. Two weeks later Lloyds TSB informed him that his application had been unsuccessful. He knew that there had been thousands of applications and he was not surprised to have had his submission rejected.

Undeterred, Glynn searched for Paralympic partners and found Sainsbury's. Glynn discovered that they were also inviting nominations and he didn't hesitate to apply. After six weeks Sainsbury's replied, accepting the nomination. Lisa and Mark were contacted and so started the process of verifying Alby's situation and making the arrangements for Alby to carry the torch. The torch would be reasonably heavy and although Alby had regained much of his strength, carrying the torch for a third of a mile would be far too much for him. It was decided that Glynn would accompany Alby to offer what help he could.

There seemed to be so much to organise. Where exactly would Alby carry the torch? At what time would it happen? Who would go to London with him? Would accommodation be provided? Little by little, the information filtered through to Lisa and Mark. The Paralympic torch would be relayed throughout the night, unlike the Olympic torch, which was only carried during the day. Alby's slot was 1.00am in north London. Glynn discovered that Alby would be one of a cohort of six torch bearers and was delighted to learn that Alby had been given a very special place in that team. He was going to be the one to light the lamp that would take the flame on the next stage of its journey.

The Romford Recorder, the Essex Chronicle and the Watford Observer were just some of the newspapers that carried the story. The school newsletter carried the news of this once in a lifetime opportunity that had been given to their Alby. He became known as Albus Dobindore and his Torch of Fire – a loose reference to the Harry Potter character of Albus Dumbledore and the book, Harry Potter and the Goblet of Fire.

Mark

"We just couldn't believe it when we learned that Albs was going to be carrying the torch. Two years earlier he couldn't walk! It was the cherry on the top of the cake for us. It was almost as if someone else had recognised what we already knew – that Alby was a lad who had achieved the impossible. We asked Glynn to accompany him. We knew Albs would need support, both physically and emotionally, and we knew that Glynn would look after him.

"Things were very slow to get going. We had to send Alby's measurements to the organisers because both Glynn and Alby had to wear special Paralympic white suits. They looked quite striking, especially the trousers, which bore a bright blue flash but, right at the last minute, the trouser design was changed to all white. Compared with the original ones they looked plain. Alby's trousers didn't arrive until two days before the event and we were panicking that they'd got lost in the post and Alby would have to forfeit his place. That was unthinkable!"

Lisa

"So many of our friends and family members wanted to be there to support and encourage Alby. It might have only seemed a short distance to most people but Alby was only just used to walking again, never mind the distance he would cover.

"We'd been told that Alby would be given accommodation in a London hotel but he could only have one person with him so that would be me. Everyone else would meet us there."

The day before the procession, Lisa drove herself and Alby to London, where they were being put up in a hotel. Lisa was glad of that as she wasn't sure how Alby would cope with the physical demands of travelling and walking in the procession on the same day. Mark was left to organise the friends and relatives who were going later. Glynn also went to London the day before. There were six torch bearers and their supporters in the same hotel. On the day of the procession they were collected from the hotel and transported to the outskirts of Watford where their leg of the journey would start.

28 August 2012

Excitement had been building for several days – not only in Alby's house but in the whole neighbourhood. People knocked on the door to ask what time Lisa and Mark thought they should leave to make sure they were there in plenty of time and didn't miss anything. Tension started making itself felt during the afternoon.

Glynn's wife, Anne, arrived early in the evening. The house was full of the excited chatter of Alby's aunts, uncles and cousins. Mark fitted as many people as he could into his car and at 9pm a small procession of cars set out for Watford. They'd allowed plenty of time for all the usual delays that can beset a motorist – traffic jams, accidents and road works – but the journey to London was uneventful and they arrived at Sainsbury's Watford car park before 10.30pm. Alby was due at 12.50am so they had plenty of time to spare. Fortunately, the evening was dry and mild as they took up their positions along the route. Tony was there. Anna and Jacqui were there. Scott was there. Everyone who was important to Alby was there and their presence said, "We believe in you and acknowledge the achievement of your incredible journey."

All those in Alby's team were collected from the hotel at about the same time as Mark's entourage set out from Harold Wood. With a much shorter distance to cover they were on the outskirts of Watford in half an hour. Alby was the last of his team to carry the torch and would be the one arriving at their finishing point at Sainsbury's. Unfortunately, their departure was delayed as the previous team was running late. Every half hour they expected to see the earlier group and every half hour they received more reports of delays. The wait didn't seem to bother anyone. There was a party atmosphere and people passed the time talking about Alby's achievements and how privileged they felt to have been included in such a special moment. Every so often the shout went up, "Here they come!" only to subside into disappointed groans that it turned out not to be the case.

Glynn

Alby and Glynn were scheduled to arrive at their destination hours before they were due to set out but by midnight no one in their team had even started their journey. The waiting crowd was getting restless but dealt with the extended wait with good-natured enthusiasm. Eventually, at 1.00am on 29 August 2012, the team of six torch bearers and their partners set out. Alby was determined to walk his allotted distance but until his starting point was reached he needed to conserve his energy so Glynn pushed him in his wheelchair. One by one, the other five torch-bearers completed their distance and handed over the torch to the next bearer. Alby's turn to complete his third of a mile came all too quickly.

Alby saw the crowds and gasped. He'd never seen anything like it – well, only at football matches on television, but never in real life! He stood up and his wheelchair was taken by one of the Paralympic officials who walked behind Alby and Glynn. Half way through his journey Alby faltered. He'd not walked this far since the accident and was feeling the physical pain of exhaustion. He didn't know if his legs would take him any further. He hesitated and the man with his wheelchair sprang forward. "Would he like to sit down?" he asked. Alby shook his head vehemently.

"No way!" he thought, "I'm doing this!" Glynn had one arm around Alby and the other holding Alby's arm and supporting the weight of the torch. Glynn whispered words of encouragement at each step. There was an excited roar as the escort vehicles came into view at 3.00am. The noise was deafening. Alby and Glynn had a small army of supporters who, in spite of the best efforts of the official walking escorts to keep them at a distance, seemed to be crowding in on them in an attempt to shake their hands or pat them on the back. Words of encouragement were shouted over the crowd and Alby could not contain his excitement. He had taken to fame and stardom like the proverbial duck to water, and he could not stop smiling. Joy radiated from his face as he pushed himself to place one foot in front of the other, determined to complete his Olympic journey. He just had to do it. Failure most definitely was NOT an option but it didn't stop him being frightened by the enormity of it all and he began to shake. He wanted to cry although he had no idea why but that too was most definitely NOT an option.

Beads of perspiration stood out on Alby's forehead. Glynn tightened his grip as Alby leaned into him and, although Alby didn't know it, Glynn heard the sigh that escaped from Alby's lips. "You can do this Albs," said Glynn "I know you can. Lean on me. Just trust me and I'll take the weight." Alby looked at his teacher, grinned and said, "Yes sir!"

The crowd roared, "ALBY! ALBY! ALBY!" as more and more people joined those who wanted to accompany Alby to the finish. Just as someone thought they'd secured a place beside him, they were relegated to the side of the road when another person stepped out to join in. The white-clad heroes slowly made their way to finish, where the flashes of hundreds of cameras lit up the night sky. By this time the torch seemed to weigh a ton, but Glynn steadied Alby's hand as he leaned forward to light the lamp. A runner then whisked the lamp away to take the flame to the next stage of its journey. Reporters were everywhere. The names of national daily newspapers were bandied about by journalists eager to interview those closest to Alby. "How long have you known him? Has he always had difficulty walking? I hear he had an accident? Would he give us an interview?"

Mark, Lisa, Jimmy, Glynn, Anna, Jacqui – Alby looked around and beckoned everyone to join him for the photos. Lisa was crying tears of joy. "You did it," and she hugged her eldest son for as long as she thought he would let her. After all, he was a teenager, and public displays of affection from Mum were supposed to be frowned upon in, but not by Alby.

He turned to Lisa and said, "I love you, Mum." Soon it wasn't only Lisa who was crying.

Glynn and Alby in their Paralympic torch uniforms

Alby lighting his own torch

Glynn supporting Alby with the lit Paralympic torch

Alby and Lisa with the Paralympic torch

Mark, Alby, Jimmy and Lisa at the Paralympic torch ceremony

Chapter 13
Eighteen

22 September 2012

Alby kept his eyes firmly closed and listened. Nothing. He could hear the sound of traffic in the distance and he could hear the birds telling the rest of the world to wake up. But that was it. No one was up yet but at 5.00am it was what he expected. He also expected to feel different this morning. It didn't have to be a big 'different' but he had expected something. Today was supposed to be a big day. Today he was not a child anymore. Today he was 18!

Having established that he didn't feel the slightest bit different he opened his eyes and looked around his bedroom. Nothing was different. He decided that being 18 was definitely overrated. He didn't know what else would be absolutely no different that day but he did know that he was looking forward to his party. His mum had told him that about 50 people were coming along and he did love a party. He thought about it a little more and grinned. He would be the centre of attention. Alby was getting used to being the centre of attention and he revelled in it!

The banner outside the house announced Alby's birthday to the world. Once the rest of the family was awake the bustle began. "Hiya big man! How's it feel to be a proper grown up then?" Alby looked at Mark as he shuffled himself around ready to get out of bed. He shrugged his shoulders indifferently. He tried to look as though it was just another day and he wasn't in the least bit excited but he couldn't help grinning and Mark burst out laughing.

"Well, we're all excited even if you're not," he said as he prodded Alby in the side, causing him to collapse into fits of laughter.

Linda, Jim, Pauline and Bernie were the first to arrive and then Alby and Jimmy's friends started to filter in. As more people arrived the party atmosphere became charged with the electricity of uncontainable excitement for the adults and the young people. So many of those close to Alby doubted he would actually be alive on his eighteenth birthday, let alone take part in the celebrations himself.

The weather was with them – no sign of rain and a perfect day for the barbecue. First to arrive was the bouncy castle. Alby could imagine the fun that his guests would have on it and laughed to himself. He was now a proper grown-up and most of his guests would be proper grown-ups too but they would love playing on a bouncy castle, just like five year olds. Next to arrive was the inflatable goal. There would be plenty of football enthusiasts who would be delighted with that particular piece of fun but later they found that most people couldn't get a look in when Granddad Jim and Jimmy started shooting goals!

For those brave enough to try it, a slide, a stumble and a trip along the greased pole would provide plenty of entertainment for the other guests. Two people trying to knock each other off the pole was not for the fainthearted and Alby thought it would be amusing to wait until some of his guests had had a few beers and then persuade them to try it.

By early afternoon the burgers, sausages and chicken were ready for the barbecue. The candy floss machine was whirring and Alby's huge football birthday cake presided over everything else on the food table. Ten staff from Shenfield High School and forty of Alby's friends and family filled the garden. The beer, the wine and the laughter flowed freely and Alby enjoyed himself more than he thought possible. Most of his peers had tiptoed into the shallows of alcohol long before their eighteenth birthdays and some had even swum along to the deep end but Alby's confinement to hospitals had kept him well and truly dry. So, Alby had his first taste of lager on his birthday and it wasn't an experiment he was keen to repeat. He thought it tasted disgusting!

The partying continued long into the night. Alby, centre of attention and loving every minute of it, received compliments and admiration as if he was a king being paid homage by his subjects. He enjoyed the noise, the laughter, the attention and considered himself lucky to have such a wonderful family and so many friends. There was more than one guest there that evening who saw that Alby didn't realise what a profound effect he had on others.

Chapter 14
Friends?

Lisa put the phone down and closed her eyes. She could feel the tears behind her eyelids, willing them to go back to where they had come from, but it was too late. One tear escaped and began its rapid descent down her cheek. Sometimes Mark asked Lisa for a glass of water and she delighted in filling it so full that it was difficult to move. Only surface tension held the fluid in check but once the balance was tipped, once that tension was broken, it was like opening flood gates. So it was with Lisa's tears. Once the first rebellious drop had defied her instructions, the rest followed in ludicrously quick succession. Lisa was beyond upset and had reached the next level – anger. The phone call had ignited her blue touch paper and Lisa let the anger wash over here. *Three times,* she thought, *three damned times!* When someone you've known for years turns down an invitation to get together you accept that that sort of thing happens. People have busy lives. The second time Lisa reminded Sarah and Mike that they had not been out in a foursome for months, she gave them a choice of dates. They couldn't make any of them. Lisa (trusting, naïve, super-idiot as she called herself) then tried again. School events, very important shopping trips, work socials and family commitments – the list was endless. Lisa asked Sarah to ring her when her, Mike's or the children's interminably long list of engagements gave them just one small window, which obviously didn't have to occupy a whole evening. Just a couple of hours to catch up would be good. Neither Lisa nor Mark ever heard from Sarah or Mike again.

When a family has been through something as gut-wrenchingly traumatic and life-changing as Lisa and Mark, it becomes really important for them to know that not everything in their world has changed. They thought that friends would be the one constant in their ever changing existence. Sarah and Mike were not the first and Lisa just knew they wouldn't be the last of their friends to drift away from their relationship. Her suspicion regarding the reason behind her friends' callous and thoughtless behaviour was confirmed later when Lisa bumped into a friend who had not abandoned her to the constantly changing existence that had become her and Mark's life. "Laura saw Sarah a couple of weeks ago and asked after you. She knew how close the four of you had been and was speechless when she found out you'd not seen them. From the rest of the conversation it turns out that they feel awkward. Apparently they don't know what to say. They feel guilty about having two healthy children." Lisa was dumbfounded.

"Healthy!" she exploded, "Healthy! Alby hasn't got a bloody disease! He's had an accident! It was a horrible, unfair, stupid, bloody accident!" Lisa closed her eyes but this time all she felt was anger and this time without the tears. If she was honest with herself she acknowledged that her and Mark's social circle had probably halved since The Accident. Rather than support them and admit that they found it difficult to find the right words, so many people decided it was easier to just avoid seeing Lisa and Mark and thereby avoid dealing with feeling uncomfortable. Lisa had to admit to herself that she was losing the patience to make excuses for the treatment they had received from some people. These people, she reasoned, are not children, unskilled in diplomacy and possibly even empathy, but adults who should know better. "Why don't people just tell us that they don't know what to say? Why don't they just say that they feel awkward and they know there is nothing they can do except just be there for us. That would be enough for us, wouldn't it Mark?"

Mark sighed, put his arm round her, pulled her close to him and said nothing. He knew how she felt because he felt it too. "It's nothing short of cruelty," he thought. Lisa turned to face him but he could see she wasn't looking at him. She had that faraway look which meant that thoughts were whirring away in her head.

"People ought to be issued with a handbook when something awful happens to someone they know. That way, people like us wouldn't end up being hurt by the very people we thought we could rely on."

Mark smiled. He was sure there would be lots of stuff like that out there already but he asked, "What would you like it to say?" Lisa outlined her idea.

"There would be an introductory section specifying that the book is for anyone who has a friend/relative/acquaintance who has gone through something life-changing or dramatic or awful."

Lisa raised the thumb on her left hand, touching its tip with her right index finger, changing to the next finger as she counted off her new rules to Mark.

"Rule 1: Unless you are completely devoid of any feelings whatsoever, DO NOT AVOID THEM. This includes crossing over to the other side of the road; not ringing them; ringing them when you know they're unlikely to be there and not leaving a message; refusing their invitations; not issuing your own invitations to them.

"Rule 2: Having followed Rule 1, you should show them that you care (on the assumption that you do, of course) and you should GO OUT OF YOUR WAY TO SEE THEM.

"Rule 3: Having followed Rule 2, (because you obviously do care) unless you have been through EXACTLY what they have been through, DO NOT SAY, 'I know how you feel,' because, believe me, you do not.

"Rule 4: In fact, tell them the exact opposite – but don't begin your sentence with 'I'. Remember, it's not about YOU, it's about them, so 'It must be so hard for you' is a good place to start, followed by something like 'It's impossible to know how you feel but it must be awful/devastating/horrible/shitty, etc.' (whatever would be your normal mode of speech).

"Rule 5: Offer to do anything that would make their life easier and then suggest something that you know you would do – some shopping, mind the children, etc whilst they try and organise their life around what has happened or perhaps just sit there and listen to the talk about the unfairness of their situation."

Lisa swapped her counting hand and continued.

"Rule 6: Don't offer clichés like 'Time is a great healer' or 'Well, at least you've got…' No one's life is ever 'healed' after a life-changing trauma. It will always leave a scar. The best they can hope for is to adjust to it, incorporate how they feel into some semblance of normal life. They also don't look at what they've got – whether it's other people or a fantastic holiday to look forward to. The fact is, that whatever they've got, they will still have it but with the added burden of whatever or whoever it is that they haven't got!

"Rule 7: Check with them from time to time to reassure them that you did mean your kind offer and ask if they're ready to take you up on it.

"Rule 8: If you know anyone who is likely to behave like the person lacking feelings in Rule 1 perhaps you could speak to them and give them some direction."

Lisa paused and took a deep breath.

"Sounds like a good idea," Mark responded. "I'm sure people don't intend to hurt us you know – perhaps they don't know what to say and rather than feel awkward, they just avoid us. I can't imagine that they actually know how hurt we are by their actions." Lisa frowned.

"Maybe you're right," she said, "and perhaps I should write out the Guide and then send copies of it to all the people we haven't seen since Alby's accident. Anne and Glynn went through exactly the same thing. They told me that when Glynn lost his first wife and Anne's son took his own life several people they thought of as friends just disappeared from their lives, so maybe they would like a few copies to send to all those thoughtless people!"

However hurtful or even despicable Lisa thought those actions were, she reached the inevitable conclusion that her family didn't need or even want friends like that. After all, they weren't really friends. They were just people.

Chapter 15
Return to School – Again

September 2014

Alby, like so many young people, had absolutely no idea of what he wanted to do. He'd done school and he'd done Sixth Form College. He didn't think he wanted to study any more – well, not for the time being anyway. He wanted something positive. In school he'd sat with many students with a disability. They were sometimes badly behaved. Some were rude to staff and did not show any appreciation for the help and support that members of staff offered them. Alby knew that often such behaviour was the result of frustration and anger caused by their disability but he also knew that such behaviour was a complete waste of their time and energy. He hoped he'd always responded positively to the help he'd been given and that gave him an idea. He missed the younger students with whom he'd come into contact. He had spent his free periods in the Special Educational Needs teaching area and had formed friendships with younger students who sometimes were engaged in their own struggles with their studies. Sometimes Alby helped them with their work and sometimes he just encouraged them to do their best or even just concentrate. Whatever it was, it led Alby back to Shenfield High School as a mentor. Lisa took him three days a week and the two of them supported lessons, sitting next to anyone who needed their help.

Alby had to go through the Criminal Records checks to make sure he wouldn't be a danger to the students. They were more likely to be in danger of one of Alby's famous scowls if they behaved in a way of which he disapproved. For three days a week Alby and Lisa arrived at the school at 9am and went straight to their first lesson. The students in all Alby's lessons needed help and support – some of them with their work, some with their behaviour and some with both. Alby certainly had his work cut out for him.

During a typical day for Alby, first lesson was timetabled as science and it turned out to be physics. Eight students were learning about the conductive properties of metals. Concentration levels were low and noise levels were high. 14-year-olds have high levels of energy and testosterone – not necessarily in that order. Electrons and ions were clearly not on their list of priorities that morning. Alby seated himself next to Joe who was struggling to understand what was required of him. Alby showed him what the teacher had asked students to do and the boy settled to the task. During the lesson, one or two of the boys called out with questions or comments, some relevant and some not. Alby frowned and order was restored.

The teacher was trying desperately to make himself heard above the cacophony of nine students full of excitement because they were going to be 'doing a practical.' That meant being engaged in a practical activity which meant the hands-on use of equipment, maybe chemicals, maybe fire and possibly even causing explosions or smells – and that was if everything went to plan. If it went wrong the sky could literally be the limit. Students were looking at the conductive properties of metals and Sir insisted on some notes being made in exercise books before any practical work could even be thought about. The girl Alby was sitting with was having trouble deciding what to write down first. The information on the whiteboard screen was arranged in blocks. That was a great way to learn small chunks of information but could leave students confused about the order in which the information should be recorded. Alby patiently pointed to the order in which Megan should be making her notes.

When the time came for the practical part of the lesson, students were expected to work in pairs, so Alby took a back seat, a seat that was nearly knocked over by Joe when he decided to run and look at another student's result. Running in a science laboratory is strictly taboo and Alby insisted Joe return to his own seat.

The next lesson was English. The class comprised mostly the same students who'd been in the previous lesson. The lesson began with a Word search, which was a particular favourite with them. Lisa was banned from taking part because she always completed them far quicker than any of the students but somehow a copy found its way into her hands. She'd made rapid progress with it when it was snatched away from her by the teacher, amid much laughter from the students. Lisa was in the class because she had to drive Alby to school and she was able to offer help to some of the students too. It seemed that Alby had the same ability with word searches as his mother and Megan was benefiting again from his help. The next part of the lesson focussed on the structure of letter writing and the protocols involved in writing particular types of letter, e.g. a letter of complaint or a letter of enquiry. Alby helped the students to write their letters using the formula they'd been given.

History followed after break and the teacher produced some photographs from the Second World War. Students had to examine the photographs and decide if they could be considered a reliable source of evidence. Once more, Alby helped to keep the students focussed and on track with their task.

Lisa sat at the back of the classroom and thought back to the accident. She pondered on how far Alby had come – against all the odds, all the warnings and all the predictions. He'd just gone and shown them all how wrong they were. Who knew how much further he would go?

Chapter 16
Living with Me

I wanted to make a personal contribution to this book (as if the fact that it's basically about me wasn't enough) but when it came to the crunch I realised it was easier said than done.

Many people have asked me if I remember anything about The Accident and I don't. In fact, I don't remember anything at all that happened on the day of The Accident. I only remember stuff that happened before then and quite a long time after it. So, all the dramas that you've been reading about completely passed me by. I knew nothing about my family's anguish concerning my injuries, their anxiety waiting for news and their elation when I made progress.

The first thing I remember post-Accident was at The Children's Trust, when Mum was standing outside with another social outcast, otherwise known as a smoker. I have a memory of seeing the two of them smoking and talking. Mum always had the ability to put the world to rights and she seemed to have a better quality of ideas when she had a ciggie in her hand. I would like to emphasise that Mum does not smoke now, something of which she can be very proud. I hated seeing her smoking. I didn't like it before The Accident – couldn't stand the horrible smell. But when you've experienced a Close Encounter like I have, you realise that people who deliberately put life-threatening chemical cocktails into their bodies are just nuts!

Since the Tadworth Day of Remembering, recollections of my time in hospital were patchy. Once I came home for good and life settled down, I felt pretty much back to normal – well, at least in the memory department.

I loved going back to school. I won't deny that I very much enjoyed being the star attraction. Being that much older when I returned to school I realised that life there could be a trifle boring and I did my best to liven things up. Sometimes I managed to get away with it and sometimes I didn't. Speeding in the electric wheelchair was just the best thing ever! I did get properly done for it but they just wrote a stroppy note to Mum in my planner. It was quite funny that they wanted me to be treated just like any other student but I often wasn't and I just loved it!

Being classed as disabled opened up a whole new world to me. Friendships were the first thing to come under the spotlight. Harry, Charlie, Anoop, Tyler and George were the best mates I could have had. They spent their break times with me and whether we stayed indoors or went outside we had a great laugh. When I got back onto my feet a bit, we even played football outside and no, they didn't always let me win. In the good weather, when the school police allowed us onto the playing field, Tyler and I had wheelchair races. I always won. Tyler reckoned it was because my wheelchair was electric and his wasn't but I told him it was just because he was a wimp. Other people that I thought were friends just seemed to evaporate into thin air. That happened with some of Mum and Mark's friends too but I tried not to let it bother me the way that I saw it upset Mum.

My first real experience of Living with a Disability was when I had two weeks of work experience and I had to go somewhere that either had lift access or work I could do on the ground floor. Most places are geared up to make pretty much all areas accessible for wheelchair users, but some older buildings haven't been able to make the necessary alterations. For the time being, members of my family take me where I need to go but I guess when the time comes for me to try independent living I might find some inaccessibility frustrating.

I can do a lot more than anyone thought I would be able to do but Mum still gets upset about what I can't do. At times like that I put my arm round her and tell her that it doesn't bother me, so she didn't ought to let it bother her. But everyone knows what mums are like!

I know I could do more and when I eventually go for independent living I hope to have an assistance dog to help me live a normal life. I've seen what those wonderful dogs can do and what a huge difference they make to someone like me.

For now I'm happy going back to school to help students who need support and encouragement. I have a very loving and supportive family and a devoted dog. I play football and I go horse riding, which I love. My life is different from what it would have been if The Accident hadn't happened, but it's a good life, it's MY life and I like it!

Love always, Alby

Epilogue

Glynn Bentley met Alby Dobinson at Shenfield High School and heard his amazing story. He later told his wife about the incredible young man he'd met and Anne said she'd love to write Alby's touching story. Later, Lisa Walsh, Alby's mum, told Glynn she wished someone would write Alby's story. Anne later met Alby when she started teaching at the same school and the rest, as they say, is history.

The decision was made that it would not just be an account of events but would be the story, complete with the emotion, elation, laughter, sadness, disappointment and joy felt by most people every day. The resulting collaboration is this book, which was not a sprint but very much a marathon, which took much longer than anticipated to complete.

The author's son Stuart read the preliminary draft of the first two chapters and loved it, having met Alby at the wedding of his mum and Glynn. In May 2012, due to increasing mental health difficulties, Stuart took his own life. Only those who have suffered this type of loss know what a very traumatic form of bereavement it is and, unfortunately, work on this book ceased temporarily.

Eventually, work began again and the author collaborated with Mark Walsh, Alby's stepdad. His input was invaluable, especially when Lisa found it hard to speak about events. In 2014, Mark was treated for skin cancer. Although he appeared to make a full recovery, it returned and in August 2016 Mark passed away. His widow, Alby's mum Lisa, found she had another steep hill of grief to climb.

Both families are still learning to live with grief, loss and change. Life is very different for everyone involved but it is